Mysticism and Logic and Other Essays
Russell, Bertrand

About Russell:

Bertrand Arthur William Russell, 3rd Earl Russell, OM, FRS (18 May 1872 – 2 February 1970), was a British philosopher, logician, mathematician, historian, religious sceptic, social reformer, socialist and pacifist. Although he spent the majority of his life in England, he was born in Wales, where he also died. Russell led the British "revolt against idealism" in the early 1900s and is considered one of the founders of analytic philosophy along with his protégé Wittgenstein and his elder Frege. He co-authored, with A. N. Whitehead, Principia Mathematica, an attempt to ground mathematics on logic. His philosophical essay "On Denoting" has been considered a "paradigm of philosophy." Both works have had a considerable influence on logic, mathematics, set theory, linguistics and analytic philosophy. He was a prominent anti-war activist, championing free trade between nations and anti-imperialism. Russell was imprisoned for his pacifist activism during World War I, campaigned against Adolf Hitler, for nuclear disarmament, criticised Soviet totalitarianism and the United States of America's involvement in the Vietnam War. In 1950, Russell was awarded the Nobel Prize in Literature, "in recognition of his varied and significant writings in which he champions humanitarian ideals and freedom of thought."

Preface

The following essays have been written and published at various times, and my thanks are due to the previous publishers for the permission to reprint them.

The essay on "Mysticism and Logic" appeared in the *Hibbert Journal* for July, 1914. "The Place of Science in a Liberal Education" appeared in two numbers of *The New Statesman*, May 24 and 31, 1913. "The Free Man's Worship" and "The Study of Mathematics" were included in a former collection (now out of print), *Philosophical Essays*, also published by Messrs. Longmans, Green & Co. Both were written in 1902; the first appeared originally in the *Independent Review* for 1903, the second in the *New Quarterly*, November, 1907. In theoretical Ethics, the position advocated in "The Free Man's Worship" is not quite identical with that which I hold now: I feel less convinced than I did then of the objectivity of good and evil. But the general attitude towards life which is suggested in that essay still seems to me, in the main, the one which must be adopted in times of stress and difficulty by those who have no dogmatic religious beliefs, if inward defeat is to be avoided.

The essay on "Mathematics and the Metaphysicians" was written in 1901, and appeared in an American magazine, *The International Monthly*, under the title "Recent Work in the Philosophy of Mathematics." Some points in this essay require modification in view of later work. These are indicated in footnotes. Its tone is partly explained by the fact that the editor begged me to make the article "as romantic as possible."

All the above essays are entirely popular, but those that follow are somewhat more technical. "On Scientific Method in Philosophy" was the Herbert Spencer lecture at Oxford in 1914, and was published by the Clarendon Press, which has kindly allowed me to include it in this collection. "The Ultimate Constituents of Matter" was an address to the Manchester Philosophical Society, early in 1915, and was published in the *Monist* in July of that year. The essay on "The Relation of Sense-data to Physics" was written in January, 1914, and first appeared in No. 4 of that year's volume of *Scientia*, an International Review of Scientific Synthesis, edited by M. Eugenio Rignano, published monthly by Messrs. Williams and Norgate,

London, Nicola Zanichelli, Bologna, and Félix Alcan, Paris. The essay "On the Notion of Cause" was the presidential address to the Aristotelian Society in November, 1912, and was published in their *Proceedings* for 1912-13. "Knowledge by Acquaintance and Knowledge by Description" was also a paper read before the Aristotelian Society, and published in their *Proceedings* for 1910-11.

London,
September, 1917

Chapter 1

Mysticism and Logic

Metaphysics, or the attempt to conceive the world as a whole by means of thought, has been developed, from the first, by the union and conflict of two very different human impulses, the one urging men towards mysticism, the other urging them towards science. Some men have achieved greatness through one of these impulses alone, others through the other alone: in Hume, for example, the scientific impulse reigns quite unchecked, while in Blake a strong hostility to science co-exists with profound mystic insight. But the greatest men who have been philosophers have felt the need both of science and of mysticism: the attempt to harmonise the two was what made their life, and what always must, for all its arduous uncertainty, make philosophy, to some minds, a greater thing than either science or religion.

Before attempting an explicit characterisation of the scientific and the mystical impulses, I will illustrate them by examples from two philosophers whose greatness lies in the very intimate blending which they achieved. The two philosophers I mean are Heraclitus and Plato.

Heraclitus, as every one knows, was a believer in universal flux: time builds and destroys all things. From the few fragments that remain, it is not easy to discover how he arrived at his opinions, but there are some sayings that strongly suggest scientific observation as the source.

"The things that can be seen, heard, and learned," he says, "are what I prize the most." This is the language of the empiricist, to whom observation is the sole guarantee of truth. "The sun is new every day," is another fragment; and this opinion, in spite of its paradoxical character, is obviously inspired by scientific reflection, and no doubt seemed to him to obviate the difficulty of understanding how the sun can work its way underground from west to east during the night. Actual observation must also have suggested to him his central doctrine, that Fire is the one permanent substance, of which all visible things are passing phases. In combustion we see things change utterly, while their flame and heat rise up into the air and vanish.

"This world, which is the same for all," he says, "no one of gods or men has made; but it was ever, is now, and ever shall be, an ever-living Fire, with measures kindling, and measures going out."

"The transformations of Fire are, first of all, sea; and half of the sea is earth, half whirlwind."

This theory, though no longer one which science can accept, is nevertheless scientific in spirit. Science, too, might have inspired the famous saying to which Plato alludes: "You cannot step twice into the same rivers; for fresh waters are ever flowing in upon you." But we find also another statement among the extant fragments: "We step and do not step into the same rivers; we are and are not."

The comparison of this statement, which is mystical, with the one quoted by Plato, which is scientific, shows how intimately the two tendencies are blended in the system of Heraclitus. Mysticism is, in essence, little more than a certain intensity and depth of feeling in regard to what is believed about the universe; and this kind of feeling leads Heraclitus, on the basis of his science, to strangely poignant sayings concerning life and the world, such as:

"Time is a child playing draughts, the kingly power is a child's."

It is poetic imagination, not science, which presents Time as despotic lord of the world, with all the irresponsible frivolity of a child. It is mysticism, too, which leads Heraclitus to assert the identity of opposites: "Good and ill are one," he says; and again: "To God all things are fair and good and right, but men hold some things wrong and some right."

Much of mysticism underlies the ethics of Heraclitus. It is true that a scientific determinism alone might have inspired the statement: "Man's character is his fate"; but only a mystic would have said:

"Every beast is driven to the pasture with blows"; and again:

"It is hard to fight with one's heart's desire. Whatever it wishes to get, it purchases at the cost of soul"; and again:

"Wisdom is one thing. It is to know the thought by which all things are steered through all things."[1]

Examples might be multiplied, but those that have been given are enough to show the character of the man: the facts of science, as they appeared to him, fed the flame in his soul, and in its light he saw into the depths of the world by the reflection of his own dancing swiftly penetrating fire. In such a nature we see the true union of the mystic and the man of science—the highest eminence, as I think, that it is possible to achieve in the world of thought.

In Plato, the same twofold impulse exists, though the mystic impulse is distinctly the stronger of the two, and secures ultimate victory whenever the conflict is sharp. His description of the cave is the classical statement of belief in a knowledge and reality truer and more real than that of the senses:
<

div class="block">

"Imagine [2] a number of men living in an underground cavernous chamber, with an entrance open to the light, extending along the entire length of the cavern, in which they have been confined, from their childhood, with their legs and necks so shackled that they are obliged to sit still and look straight forwards, because their chains render it impossible for them to turn their heads round: and imagine a bright fire burning some way off, above and behind them, and an elevated roadway passing between the fire and the prisoners, with a low wall built along it, like the screens which conjurors put up in front of their audience, and above which they exhibit their wonders.

I have it, he replied.

Also figure to yourself a number of persons walking behind this wall, and carrying with them statues of men, and images of other animals, wrought in wood and stone and all kinds of materials, together with various other articles, which overtop the wall; and, as you might expect, let some of the passers-by be talking, and others silent.

You are describing a strange scene, and strange prisoners.

They resemble us, I replied.

Now consider what would happen if the course of nature brought them a release from their fetters, and a remedy for their foolishness, in the following manner. Let us suppose that one of them has been released, and compelled suddenly to stand up, and turn his neck round and walk with open eyes towards the light; and let us suppose that he goes through all these actions with pain, and that the dazzling splendour renders him incapable of discerning those objects of which he used formerly to see the shadows. What answer should you expect him to make, if some one were to tell him that in those days he was watching foolish phantoms, but that now he is somewhat nearer to reality, and is turned towards things more real, and sees more correctly; above all, if he were to point out to him the several objects that are passing by, and question him, and compel him to answer what they are? Should you not expect him to be puzzled, and to regard his old visions as truer than the objects now forced upon his notice?

Yes, much truer... .

Hence, I suppose, habit will be necessary to enable him to perceive objects in that upper world. At first he will be most successful in distinguishing shadows; then he will discern the reflections of men and other things in water, and afterwards the realities; and after this he will raise his eyes to encounter the light of the moon and stars, finding it less difficult to study the heavenly bodies and the heaven itself by night, than the sun and the sun's light by day.

Doubtless.

Last of all, I imagine, he will be able to observe and contemplate the nature of the sun, not as it *appears* in water or on alien ground, but as it is in itself in its own territory.

Of course.

His next step will be to draw the conclusion, that the sun is the author of the seasons and the years, and the guardian of all things in the visible world, and in a manner the cause of all those things which he and his companions used to see.

Obviously, this will be his next step... .

Now this imaginary case, my dear Glancon, you must apply in all its parts to our former statements, by comparing the region which the eye reveals, to the prison house, and the light of the fire therein to the power of the sun: and if, by the upward

ascent and the contemplation of the upper world, you understand the mounting of the soul into the intellectual region, you
will hit the tendency of my own surmises, since you desire to
be told what they are; though, indeed, God only knows whether
they are correct. But, be that as it may, the view which I take
of the subject is to the following effect. In the world of knowledge, the essential Form of Good is the limit of our enquiries,
and can barely be perceived; but, when perceived, we cannot
help concluding that it is in every case the source of all that is
bright and beautiful,—in the visible world giving birth to light
and its master, and in the intellectual world dispensing, immediately and with full authority, truth and reason;—and that
whosoever would act wisely, either in private or in public, must
set this Form of Good before his eyes."

But in this passage, as throughout most of Plato's teaching,
there is an identification of the good with the truly real, which
became embodied in the philosophical tradition, and is still
largely operative in our own day. In thus allowing a legislative
function to the good, Plato produced a divorce between philosophy and science, from which, in my opinion, both have
suffered ever since and are still suffering. The man of science,
whatever his hopes may be, must lay them aside while he studies nature; and the philosopher, if he is to achieve truth must
do the same. Ethical considerations can only legitimately appear when the truth has been ascertained: they can and should
appear as determining our feeling towards the truth, and our
manner of ordering our lives in view of the truth, but not as
themselves dictating what the truth is to be.

There are passages in Plato—among those which illustrate
the scientific side of his mind—where he seems clearly aware
of this. The most noteworthy is the one in which Socrates, as a
young man, is explaining the theory of ideas to Parmenides.

After Socrates has explained that there is an idea of the
good, but not of such things as hair and mud and dirt, Parmenides advises him "not to despise even the meanest things," and
this advice shows the genuine scientific temper. It is with this
impartial temper that the mystic's apparent insight into a higher reality and a hidden good has to be combined if philosophy
is to realise its greatest possibilities. And it is failure in this respect that has made so much of idealistic philosophy thin,

lifeless, and insubstantial. It is only in marriage with the world that our ideals can bear fruit: divorced from it, they remain barren. But marriage with the world is not to be achieved by an ideal which shrinks from fact, or demands in advance that the world shall conform to its desires.

Parmenides himself is the source of a peculiarly interesting strain of mysticism which pervades Plato's thought—the mysticism which may be called "logical" because it is embodied in theories on logic. This form of mysticism, which appears, so far as the West is concerned, to have originated with Parmenides, dominates the reasonings of all the great mystical metaphysicians from his day to that of Hegel and his modern disciples. Reality, he says, is uncreated, indestructible, unchanging, indivisible; it is "immovable in the bonds of mighty chains, without beginning and without end; since coming into being and passing away have been driven afar, and true belief has cast them away." The fundamental principle of his inquiry is stated in a sentence which would not be out of place in Hegel: "Thou canst not know what is not—that is impossible—nor utter it; for it is the same thing that can be thought and that can be." And again: "It needs must be that what can be thought and spoken of is; for it is possible for it to be, and it is not possible for what is nothing to be." The impossibility of change follows from this principle; for what is past can be spoken of, and therefore, by the principle, still is.

Mystical philosophy, in all ages and in all parts of the world, is characterised by certain beliefs which are illustrated by the doctrines we have been considering.

There is, first, the belief in insight as against discursive analytic knowledge: the belief in a way of wisdom, sudden, penetrating, coercive, which is contrasted with the slow and fallible study of outward appearance by a science relying wholly upon the senses. All who are capable of absorption in an inward passion must have experienced at times the strange feeling of unreality in common objects, the loss of contact with daily things, in which the solidity of the outer world is lost, and the soul seems, in utter loneliness, to bring forth, out of its own depths, the mad dance of fantastic phantoms which have hitherto appeared as independently real and living. This is the negative side of the mystic's initiation: the doubt concerning common knowledge, preparing the way for the reception of what seems a higher wisdom. Many men to whom this negative experience is familiar do not pass beyond it, but for the mystic it is merely the gateway to an ampler world.

The mystic insight begins with the sense of a mystery unveiled, of a hidden wisdom now suddenly become certain beyond the possibility of a doubt. The sense of certainty and revelation comes earlier than any definite belief. The definite beliefs at which mystics arrive are the result of reflection upon the inarticulate experience gained in the moment of insight. Often, beliefs which have no real connection with this moment become subsequently attracted into the central nucleus; thus in addition to the convictions which all mystics share, we find, in many of them, other convictions of a more local and temporary character, which no doubt become amalgamated with what was essentially mystical in virtue of their subjective certainty. We may ignore such inessential accretions, and confine ourselves to the beliefs which all mystics share.

The first and most direct outcome of the moment of illumination is belief in the possibility of a way of knowledge which may be called revelation or insight or intuition, as contrasted with sense, reason, and analysis, which are regarded as blind guides leading to the morass of illusion. Closely connected with this belief is the conception of a Reality behind the world of appearance and utterly different from it. This Reality is regarded with an admiration often amounting to worship; it is felt to be always and everywhere close at hand, thinly veiled by the shows of sense, ready, for the receptive mind, to shine in its glory even through the apparent folly and wickedness of Man. The poet, the artist, and the lover are seekers after that glory: the haunting beauty that they pursue is the faint reflection of its sun. But the mystic lives in the full light of the vision: what others dimly seek he knows, with a knowledge beside which all other knowledge is ignorance.

The second characteristic of mysticism is its belief in unity, and its refusal to admit opposition or division anywhere. We found Heraclitus saying "good and ill are one"; and again he says, "the way up and the way down is one and the same." The same attitude appears in the simultaneous assertion of contradictory propositions, such as: "We step and do not step into the same rivers; we are and are not." The assertion of Parmenides, that reality is one and indivisible, comes from the same impulse towards unity. In Plato, this impulse is less prominent, being held in check by his theory of ideas; but it reappears, so far as his logic permits, in the doctrine of the primacy of the Good.

A third mark of almost all mystical metaphysics is the denial of the reality of Time. This is an outcome of the denial of division; if all is one, the distinction of past and future must be illusory. We have seen this doctrine prominent in Parmenides; and among moderns it is fundamental in the systems of Spinoza and Hegel.

The last of the doctrines of mysticism which we have to consider is its belief that all evil is mere appearance, an illusion produced by the divisions and oppositions of the analytic intellect. Mysticism does not maintain that such things as cruelty, for example, are good, but it denies that they are real: they belong to that lower world of phantoms from which we are to be liberated by the insight of the vision. Sometimes—for example in Hegel, and at least verbally in Spinoza—not only evil, but good also, is regarded as illusory, though nevertheless the emotional attitude towards what is held to be Reality is such as would naturally be associated with the belief that Reality is good. What is, in all cases, ethically characteristic of mysticism is absence of indignation or protest, acceptance with joy, disbelief in the ultimate truth of the division into two hostile camps, the good and the bad. This attitude is a direct outcome of the nature of the mystical experience: with its sense of unity is associated a feeling of infinite peace. Indeed it may be suspected that the feeling of peace produces, as feelings do in dreams, the whole system of associated beliefs which make up the body of mystic doctrine. But this is a difficult question, and one on which it cannot be hoped that mankind will reach agreement.

Four questions thus arise in considering the truth or falsehood of mysticism, namely:
<
    div class="block">

I. Are there two ways of knowing, which may be called respectively reason and intuition? And if so, is either to be preferred to the other?

II. Is all plurality and division illusory?

III. Is time unreal?

IV. What kind of reality belongs to good and evil?

On all four of these questions, while fully developed mysticism seems to me mistaken, I yet believe that, by sufficient restraint, there is an element of wisdom to be learned from the mystical way of feeling, which does not seem to be attainable in any other manner. If this is the truth, mysticism is to be commended as an attitude towards life, not as a creed about the world. The meta-physical creed, I shall maintain, is a mistaken outcome of the emotion, although this emotion, as colouring and informing all other thoughts and feelings, is the inspirer of whatever is best in Man. Even the cautious and patient investigation of truth by science, which seems the very antithesis of the mystic's swift certainty, may be fostered and nourished by that very spirit of reverence in which mysticism lives and moves.

I. Reason and Intuition

[3]

Of the reality or unreality of the mystic's world I know nothing. I have no wish to deny it, nor even to declare that the insight which reveals it is not a genuine insight. What I do wish to maintain—and it is here that the scientific attitude becomes imperative—is that insight, untested and unsupported, is an insufficient guarantee of truth, in spite of the fact that much of the most important truth is first suggested by its means. It is common to speak of an opposition between instinct and reason; in the eighteenth century, the opposition was drawn in favour of reason, but under the influence of Rousseau and the romantic movement instinct was given the preference, first by those who rebelled against artificial forms of government and thought, and then, as the purely rationalistic defence of traditional theology became increasingly difficult, by all who felt in science a menace to creeds which they associated with a spiritual outlook on life and the world. Bergson, under the name of "intuition," has raised instinct to the position of sole arbiter of metaphysical truth. But in fact the opposition of instinct and reason is mainly illusory. Instinct, intuition, or insight is what first leads to the beliefs which subsequent reason confirms or confutes; but the confirmation, where it is possible, consists, in the last analysis, of agreement with other beliefs no less instinctive. Reason is a harmonising, controlling force rather than a creative one. Even in the most purely logical realm, it is insight that first arrives at what is new.

Where instinct and reason do sometimes conflict is in regard to single beliefs, held instinctively, and held with such determination that no degree of inconsistency with other beliefs leads to their abandonment. Instinct, like all human faculties, is liable to error. Those in whom reason is weak are often unwilling to admit this as regards themselves, though all admit it in regard to others. Where instinct is least liable to error is in practical matters as to which right judgment is a help to survival: friendship and hostility in others, for instance, are often felt with extraordinary discrimination through very careful disguises. But even in such matters a wrong impression may be given by reserve or flattery; and in matters less directly practical, such as philosophy deals with, very strong instinctive beliefs are sometimes wholly mistaken, as we may come to know through their perceived inconsistency with other equally strong beliefs. It is such considerations that necessitate the harmonising mediation of reason, which tests our beliefs by their mutual compatibility, and examines, in doubtful cases, the possible sources of error on the one side and on the other. In this there is no opposition to instinct as a whole, but only to blind reliance upon some one interesting aspect of instinct to the exclusion of other more commonplace but not less trustworthy aspects. It is such one-sidedness, not instinct itself, that reason aims at correcting.

These more or less trite maxims may be illustrated by application to Bergson's advocacy of "intuition" as against "intellect." There are, he says, "two profoundly different ways of knowing a thing. The first implies that we move round the object: the second that we enter into it. The first depends on the point of view at which we are placed and on the symbols by which we express ourselves. The second neither depends on a point of view nor relies on any symbol. The first kind of knowledge may be said to stop at the *relative*; the second, in those cases where it is possible, to attain the *absolute*."[4] The second of these, which is intuition, is, he says, "the kind of *intellectual sympathy* by which one places oneself within an object in order to coincide with what is unique in it and therefore inexpressible" (p. 6). In illustration, he mentions self-knowledge: "there is one reality, at least, which we all seize from within, by intuition and not by simple analysis. It is our own personality in its flowing through time—our self which endures" (p. 8). The rest of Bergson's philosophy consists in reporting, through the imperfect medium of words, the knowledge gained by intuition, and the consequent complete condemnation of all the pretended knowledge derived from science and common sense.

This procedure, since it takes sides in a conflict of instinctive beliefs, stands in need of justification by proving the greater trustworthiness of the beliefs on one side than of those on the other. Bergson attempts this justification in two ways, first by explaining that intellect is a purely practical faculty to secure biological success, secondly by mentioning remarkable feats of instinct in animals and by pointing out characteristics of the world which, though intuition can apprehend them, are baffling to intellect as he interprets it.

Of Bergson's theory that intellect is a purely practical faculty, developed in the struggle for survival, and not a source of true beliefs, we may say, first, that it is only through intellect that we know of the struggle for survival and of the biological ancestry of man: if the intellect is misleading, the whole of this merely inferred history is presumably untrue. If, on the other hand, we agree with him in thinking that evolution took place as Darwin believed, then it is not only intellect, but all our faculties, that have been developed under the stress of practical utility. Intuition is seen at its best where it is directly useful, for example in regard to other people's characters and dispositions. Bergson apparently holds that capacity, for this kind of knowledge is less explicable by the struggle for existence than, for example, capacity for pure mathematics. Yet the savage deceived by false friendship is likely to pay for his mistake with his life; whereas even in the most civilised societies men are not put to death for mathematical incompetence. All the most striking of his instances of intuition in animals have a very direct survival value. The fact is, of course, that both intuition and intellect have been developed because they are useful, and that, speaking broadly, they are useful when they give truth and become harmful when they give falsehood. Intellect, in civilised man, like artistic capacity, has occasionally been developed beyond the point where it is useful to the individual; intuition, on the other hand, seems on the whole to diminish as civilisation increases. It is greater, as a rule, in children than in adults, in the uneducated than in the educated. Probably in dogs it exceeds anything to be found in human beings. But those who see in these facts a recommendation of intuition ought to return to running wild in the woods, dyeing themselves with woad and living on hips and haws.

Let us next examine whether intuition possesses any such infallibility as Bergson claims for it. The best instance of it, according to him, is our acquaintance with ourselves; yet self-knowledge is proverbially rare and difficult. Most men, for example, have in their nature meannesses, vanities, and envies of which they are quite unconscious, though even their best friends can perceive them without any difficulty. It is true that intuition has a convincingness which is lacking to intellect: while it is present, it is almost impossible to doubt its truth. But if it should appear, on examination, to be at least as fallible as intellect, its greater subjective certainty becomes a demerit, making it only the more irresistibly deceptive. Apart from self-knowledge, one of the most notable examples of intuition is the knowledge people believe themselves to possess of those with whom they are in love: the wall between different personalities seems to become transparent, and people think they see into another soul as into their own. Yet deception in such cases is constantly practised with success; and even where there is no intentional deception, experience gradually proves, as a rule, that the supposed insight was illusory, and that the slower more groping methods of the intellect are in the long run more reliable.

Bergson maintains that intellect can only deal with things in so far as they resemble what has been experienced in the past, while intuition has the power of apprehending the uniqueness and novelty that always belong to each fresh moment. That there is something unique and new at every moment, is certainly true; it is also true that this cannot be fully expressed by means of intellectual concepts. Only direct acquaintance can give knowledge of what is unique and new. But direct acquaintance of this kind is given fully in sensation, and does not require, so far as I can see, any special faculty of intuition for its apprehension. It is neither intellect nor intuition, but sensation, that supplies new data; but when the data are new in any remarkable manner, intellect is much more capable of dealing with them than intuition would be. The hen with a brood of ducklings no doubt has intuition which seems to place her inside them, and not merely to know them analytically; but when the ducklings take to the water, the whole apparent intuition is seen to be illusory, and the hen is left helpless on the shore. Intuition, in fact, is an aspect and development of instinct, and, like all instinct, is admirable in those customary surroundings which have moulded the habits of the animal in question, but totally incompetent as soon as the surroundings are changed in a way which demands some non-habitual mode of action.

The theoretical understanding of the world, which is the aim of philosophy, is not a matter of great practical importance to animals, or to savages, or even to most civilised men. It is hardly to be supposed, therefore, that the rapid, rough and ready methods of instinct or intuition will find in this field a favourable ground for their application. It is the older kinds of activity, which bring out our kinship with remote generations of animal and semi-human ancestors, that show intuition at its best. In such matters as self-preservation and love, intuition will act sometimes (though not always) with a swiftness and precision which are astonishing to the critical intellect. But philosophy is not one of the pursuits which illustrate our affinity with the past: it is a highly refined, highly civilised pursuit, demanding, for its success, a certain liberation from the life of instinct, and even, at times, a certain aloofness from all mundane hopes and fears. It is not in philosophy, therefore, that we can hope to see intuition at its best. On the contrary, since the true objects of philosophy, and the habit of thought demanded for their apprehension, are strange, unusual, and remote, it is here, more almost than anywhere else, that intellect proves superior to intuition, and that quick unanalysed convictions are least deserving of uncritical acceptance.

In advocating the scientific restraint and balance, as against the self-assertion of a confident reliance upon intuition, we are only urging, in the sphere of knowledge, that largeness of contemplation, that impersonal disinterestedness, and that freedom from practical preoccupations which have been inculcated by all the great religions of the world. Thus our conclusion, however it may conflict with the explicit beliefs of many mystics, is, in essence, not contrary to the spirit which inspires those beliefs, but rather the outcome of this very spirit as applied in the realm of thought.

II. Unity and Plurality

One of the most convincing aspects of the mystic illumination is the apparent revelation of the oneness of all things, giving rise to pantheism in religion and to monism in philosophy. An elaborate logic, beginning with Parmenides, and culminating in Hegel and his followers, has been gradually developed, to prove that the universe is one indivisible Whole, and that what seem to be its parts, if considered as substantial and self-existing, are mere illusion. The conception of a Reality quite other than the world of appearance, a reality one, indivisible, and unchanging, was introduced into Western philosophy by Parmenides, not, nominally at least, for mystical or religious reasons, but on the basis of a logical argument as to the impossibility of not-being, and most subsequent metaphysical systems are the outcome of this fundamental idea.

The logic used in defence of mysticism seems to be faulty as logic, and open to technical criticisms, which I have explained elsewhere. I shall not here repeat these criticisms, since they are lengthy and difficult, but shall instead attempt an analysis of the state of mind from which mystical logic has arisen.

Belief in a reality quite different from what appears to the senses arises with irresistible force in certain moods, which are the source of most mysticism, and of most metaphysics. While such a mood is dominant, the need of logic is not felt, and accordingly the more thoroughgoing mystics do not employ logic, but appeal directly to the immediate deliverance of their insight. But such fully developed mysticism is rare in the West. When the intensity of emotional conviction subsides, a man who is in the habit of reasoning will search for logical grounds in favour of the belief which he finds in himself. But since the belief already exists, he will be very hospitable to any ground that suggests itself. The paradoxes apparently proved by his logic are really the paradoxes of mysticism, and are the goal which he feels his logic must reach if it is to be in accordance with insight. The resulting logic has rendered most philosophers incapable of giving any account of the world of science and daily life. If they had been anxious to give such an account, they would probably have discovered the errors of their logic; but most of them were less anxious to understand the world of science and daily life than to convict it of unreality in the interests of a super-sensible "real" world.

It is in this way that logic has been pursued by those of the great philosophers who were mystics. But since they usually took for granted the supposed insight of the mystic emotion, their logical doctrines were presented with a certain dryness, and were believed by their disciples to be quite independent of the sudden illumination from which they sprang. Nevertheless their origin clung to them, and they remained—to borrow a useful word from Mr. Santayana—"malicious" in regard to the world of science and common sense. It is only so that we can account for the complacency with which philosophers have accepted the inconsistency of their doctrines with all the common and scientific facts which seem best established and most worthy of belief.

The logic of mysticism shows, as is natural, the defects which are inherent in anything malicious. The impulse to logic, not felt while the mystic mood is dominant, reasserts itself as the mood fades, but with a desire to retain the vanishing insight, or at least to prove that it *was* insight, and that what seems to contradict it is illusion. The logic which thus arises is not quite disinterested or candid, and is inspired by a certain hatred of the daily world to which it is to be applied. Such an attitude naturally does not tend to the best results. Everyone knows that to read an author simply in order to refute him is not the way to understand him; and to read the book of Nature with a conviction that it is all illusion is just as unlikely to lead to understanding. If our logic is to find the common world intelligible, it must not be hostile, but must be inspired by a genuine acceptance such as is not usually to be found among metaphysicians.

III. Time

The unreality of time is a cardinal doctrine of many metaphysical systems, often nominally based, as already by Parmenides, upon logical arguments, but originally derived, at any rate in the founders of new systems, from the certainty which is born in the moment of mystic insight. As a Persian Sufi poet says:
<
   div class="poem">
"Past and future are what veil God from our sight.
Burn up both of them with fire! How long
Wilt thou be partitioned by these segments as a reed?"[5]

The belief that what is ultimately real must be immutable is a very common one: it gave rise to the metaphysical notion of substance, and finds, even now, a wholly illegitimate satisfaction in such scientific doctrines as the conservation of energy and mass.

It is difficult to disentangle the truth and the error in this view. The arguments for the contention that time is unreal and that the world of sense is illusory must, I think, be regarded as fallacious. Nevertheless there is some sense—easier to feel than to state—in which time is an unimportant and superficial characteristic of reality. Past and future must be acknowledged to be as real as the present, and a certain emancipation from slavery to time is essential to philosophic thought. The importance of time is rather practical than theoretical, rather in relation to our desires than in relation to truth. A truer image of the world, I think, is obtained by picturing things as entering into the stream of time from an eternal world outside, than from a view which regards time as the devouring tyrant of all that is. Both in thought and in feeling, even though time be real, to realise the unimportance of time is the gate of wisdom.

That this is the case may be seen at once by asking ourselves why our feelings towards the past are so different from our feelings towards the future. The reason for this difference is wholly practical: our wishes can affect the future but not the past, the future is to some extent subject to our power, while the past is unalterably fixed. But every future will some day be past: if we see the past truly now, it must, when it was still future, have been just what we now see it to be, and what is now future must be just what we shall see it to be when it has become past. The felt difference of quality between past and future, therefore, is not an intrinsic difference, but only a difference in relation to us: to impartial contemplation, it ceases to exist. And impartiality of contemplation is, in the intellectual sphere, that very same virtue of disinterestedness which, in the sphere of action, appears as justice and unselfishness. Whoever wishes to see the world truly, to rise in thought above the tyranny of practical desires, must learn to overcome the difference of attitude towards past and future, and to survey the whole stream of time in one comprehensive vision.

The kind of way in which, as it seems to me, time ought not to enter into our theoretic philosophical thought, may be illustrated by the philosophy which has become associated with the idea of evolution, and which is exemplified by Nietzsche, pragmatism, and Bergson. This philosophy, on the basis of the development which has led from the lowest forms of life up to man, sees in *progress* the fundamental law of the universe, and thus admits the difference between *earlier* and *later* into the very citadel of its contemplative outlook. With its past and future history of the world, conjectural as it is, I do not wish to quarrel. But I think that, in the intoxication of a quick success, much that is required for a true understanding of the universe has been forgotten. Something of Hellenism, something, too, of Oriental resignation, must be combined with its hurrying Western self-assertion before it can emerge from the ardour of youth into the mature wisdom of manhood. In spite of its appeals to science, the true scientific philosophy, I think, is something more arduous and more aloof, appealing to less mundane hopes, and requiring a severer discipline for its successful practice.

Darwin's *Origin of Species* persuaded the world that the difference between different species of animals and plants is not the fixed immutable difference that it appears to be. The doctrine of natural kinds, which had rendered classification easy and definite, which was enshrined in the Aristotelian tradition, and protected by its supposed necessity for orthodox dogma, was suddenly swept away for ever out of the biological world. The difference between man and the lower animals, which to our human conceit appears enormous, was shown to be a gradual achievement, involving intermediate being who could not with certainty be placed either within or without the human family. The sun and the planets had already been shown by Laplace to be very probably derived from a primitive more or less undifferentiated nebula. Thus the old fixed landmarks became wavering and indistinct, and all sharp outlines were blurred. Things and species lost their boundaries, and none could say where they began or where they ended.

But if human conceit was staggered for a moment by its kinship with the ape, it soon found a way to reassert itself, and that way is the "philosophy" of evolution. A process which led from the am[oe]ba to Man appeared to the philosophers to be obviously a progress—though whether the am[oe]ba would agree with this opinion is not known. Hence the cycle of changes which science had shown to be the probable history of the past was welcomed as revealing a law of development towards good in the universe—an evolution or unfolding of an idea slowly embodying itself in the actual. But such a view, though it might satisfy Spencer and those whom we may call Hegelian evolutionists, could not be accepted as adequate by the more whole-hearted votaries of change. An ideal to which the world continuously approaches is, to these minds, too dead and static to be inspiring. Not only the aspiration, but the ideal too, must change and develop with the course of evolution: there must be no fixed goal, but a continual fashioning of fresh needs by the impulse which is life and which alone gives unity to the process.

Life, in this philosophy, is a continuous stream, in which all divisions are artificial and unreal. Separate things, beginnings and endings, are mere convenient fictions: there is only smooth unbroken transition. The beliefs of to-day may count as true to-day, if they carry us along the stream; but to-morrow they will be false, and must be replaced by new beliefs to meet the new situation. All our thinking consists of convenient fictions, imaginary congealings of the stream: reality flows on in spite of all our fictions, and though it can be lived, it cannot be conceived in thought. Somehow, without explicit statement, the assurance is slipped in that the future, though we cannot foresee it, will be better than the past or the present: the reader is like the child which expects a sweet because it has been told to open its mouth and shut its eyes. Logic, mathematics, physics disappear in this philosophy, because they are too "static"; what is real is no impulse and movement towards a goal which, like the rainbow, recedes as we advance, and makes every place different when it reaches it from what it appeared to be at a distance.

I do not propose to enter upon a technical examination of this philosophy. I wish only to maintain that the motives and interests which inspire it are so exclusively practical, and the problems with which it deals are so special, that it can hardly be regarded as touching any of the questions that, to my mind, constitute genuine philosophy.

The predominant interest of evolutionism is in the question of human destiny, or at least of the destiny of Life. It is more interested in morality and happiness than in knowledge for its own sake. It must be admitted that the same may be said of many other philosophies, and that a desire for the kind of knowledge which philosophy can give is very rare. But if philosophy is to attain truth, it is necessary first and foremost that philosophers should acquire the disinterested intellectual curiosity which characterises the genuine man of science. Knowledge concerning the future—which is the kind of knowledge that must be sought if we are to know about human destiny—is possible within certain narrow limits. It is impossible to say how much the limits may be enlarged with the progress of science. But what is evident is that any proposition about the future belongs by its subject-matter to some particular science, and is to be ascertained, if at all, by the methods of that science. Philosophy is not a short cut to the same kind of results as those of the other sciences: if it is to be a genuine study, it must have a province of its own, and aim at results which the other sciences can neither prove nor disprove.

Evolutionism, in basing itself upon the notion of *progress*, which is change from the worse to the better, allows the notion of time, as it seems to me, to become its tyrant rather than its servant, and thereby loses that impartiality of contemplation which is the source of all that is best in philosophic thought and feeling. Metaphysicians, as we saw, have frequently denied altogether the reality of time. I do not wish to do this; I wish only to preserve the mental outlook which inspired the denial, the attitude which, in thought, regards the past as having the same reality as the present and the same importance as the future. "In so far," says Spinoza,[6] "as the mind conceives a thing according to the dictate of reason, it will be equally affected whether the idea is that of a future, past, or present thing." It is this "conceiving according to the dictate of reason" that I find lacking in the philosophy which is based on evolution.

IV. Good and Evil

Mysticism maintains that all evil is illusory, and sometimes maintains the same view as regards good, but more often holds that all Reality is good. Both views are to be found in Heraclitus: "Good and ill are one," he says, but again, "To God all things are fair and good and right, but men hold some things wrong and some right." A similar twofold position is to be found in Spinoza, but he uses the word "perfection" when he means to speak of the good that is not merely human. "By reality and perfection I mean the same thing," he says;[7] but elsewhere we find the definition: "By *good* I shall mean that which we certainly know to be useful to us."[8] Thus perfection belongs to Reality in its own nature, but goodness is relative to ourselves and our needs, and disappears in an impartial survey. Some such distinction, I think, is necessary in order to understand the ethical outlook of mysticism: there is a lower mundane kind of good and evil, which divides the world of appearance into what seem to be conflicting parts; but there is also a higher, mystical kind of good, which belongs to Reality and is not opposed by any correlative kind of evil.

It is difficult to give a logically tenable account of this position without recognising that good and evil are subjective, that what is good is merely that towards which we have one kind of feeling, and what is evil is merely that towards which we have another kind of feeling. In our active life, where we have to exercise choice, and to prefer this to that of two possible acts, it is necessary to have a distinction of good and evil, or at least of better and worse. But this distinction, like everything pertaining to action, belongs to what mysticism regards as the world of illusion, if only because it is essentially concerned with time. In our contemplative life, where action is not called for, it is possible to be impartial, and to overcome the ethical dualism which action requires. So long as we remain *merely* impartial, we may be content to say that both the good and the evil of action are illusions. But if, as we must do if we have the mystic vision, we find the whole world worthy of love and worship, if we see

<
   div class="poem">

"The earth, and every common sight... .
Apparell'd in celestial light,"
we shall say that there is a higher good than that of action, and that this higher good belongs to the whole world as it is in reality. In this way the twofold attitude and the apparent vacillation of mysticism are explained and justified.

The possibility of this universal love and joy in all that exists is of supreme importance for the conduct and happiness of life, and gives inestimable value to the mystic emotion, apart from any creeds which may be built upon it. But if we are not to be led into false beliefs, it is necessary to realise exactly *what* the mystic emotion reveals. It reveals a possibility of human nature—a possibility of a nobler, happier, freer life than any that can be otherwise achieved. But it does not reveal anything about the non-human, or about the nature of the universe in general. Good and bad, and even the higher good that mysticism finds everywhere, are the reflections of our own emotions on other things, not part of the substance of things as they are in themselves. And therefore an impartial contemplation, freed from all pre-occupation with Self, will not judge things good or bad, although it is very easily combined with that feeling of universal love which leads the mystic to say that the whole world is good.

The philosophy of evolution, through the notion of progress, is bound up with the ethical dualism of the worse and the better, and is thus shut out, not only from the kind of survey which discards good and evil altogether from its view, but also from the mystical belief in the goodness of everything. In this way the distinction of good and evil, like time, becomes a tyrant in this philosophy, and introduces into thought the restless selectiveness of action. Good and evil, like time, are, it would seem, not general or fundamental in the world of thought, but late and highly specialised members of the intellectual hierarchy.

Although, as we saw, mysticism can be interpreted so as to agree with the view that good and evil are not intellectually fundamental, it must be admitted that here we are no longer in verbal agreement with most of the great philosophers and religious teachers of the past. I believe, however, that the elimination of ethical considerations from philosophy is both scientifically necessary and—though this may seem a paradox—an ethical advance. Both these contentions must be briefly defended.

The hope of satisfaction to our more human desires—the hope of demonstrating that the world has this or that desirable ethical characteristic—is not one which, so far as I can see, a scientific philosophy can do anything whatever to satisfy. The difference between a good world and a bad one is a difference in the particular characteristics of the particular things that exist in these worlds: it is not a sufficiently abstract difference to come within the province of philosophy. Love and hate, for example, are ethical opposites, but to philosophy they are closely analogous attitudes towards objects. The general form and structure of those attitudes towards objects which constitute mental phenomena is a problem for philosophy, but the difference between love and hate is not a difference of form or structure, and therefore belongs rather to the special science of psychology than to philosophy. Thus the ethical interests which have often inspired philosophers must remain in the background: some kind of ethical interest may inspire the whole study, but none must obtrude in the detail or be expected in the special results which are sought.

If this view seems at first sight disappointing, we may remind ourselves that a similar change has been found necessary in all the other sciences. The physicist or chemist is not now required to prove the ethical importance of his ions or atoms; the biologist is not expected to prove the utility of the plants or animals which he dissects. In pre-scientific ages this was not the case. Astronomy, for example, was studied because men believed in astrology: it was thought that the movements of the planets had the most direct and important bearing upon the lives of human beings. Presumably, when this belief decayed and the disinterested study of astronomy began, many who had found astrology absorbingly interesting decided that astronomy had too little human interest to be worthy of study. Physics, as it appears in Plato's Timæus for example, is full of ethical notions: it is an essential part of its purpose to show that the earth is worthy of admiration. The modern physicist, on the contrary, though he has no wish to deny that the earth is admirable, is not concerned, as physicist, with its ethical attributes: he is merely concerned to find out facts, not to consider whether they are good or bad. In psychology, the scientific attitude is even more recent and more difficult than in the physical sciences: it is natural to consider that human nature is either good or bad, and to suppose that the difference between good and bad, so all-important in practice, must be important in theory also. It is only during the last century that an ethically neutral psychology has grown up; and here too, ethical neutrality has been essential to scientific success.

In philosophy, hitherto, ethical neutrality has been seldom sought and hardly ever achieved. Men have remembered their wishes, and have judged philosophies in relation to their wishes. Driven from the particular sciences, the belief that the notions of good and evil must afford a key to the understanding of the world has sought a refuge in philosophy. But even from this last refuge, if philosophy is not to remain a set of pleasing dreams, this belief must be driven forth. It is a commonplace that happiness is not best achieved by those who seek it directly; and it would seem that the same is true of the good. In thought, at any rate, those who forget good and evil and seek only to know the facts are more likely to achieve good than those who view the world through the distorting medium of their own desires.

We are thus brought back to our seeming paradox, that a philosophy which does not seek to impose upon the world its own conceptions of good and evil is not only more likely to achieve truth, but is also the outcome of a higher ethical standpoint than one which, like evolutionism and most traditional systems, is perpetually appraising the universe and seeking to find in it an embodiment of present ideals. In religion, and in every deeply serious view of the world and of human destiny, there is an element of submission, a realisation of the limits of human power, which is somewhat lacking in the modern world, with its quick material successes and its insolent belief in the boundless possibilities of progress. "He that loveth his life shall lose it"; and there is danger lest, through a too confident love of life, life itself should lose much of what gives it its highest worth. The submission which religion inculcates in action is essentially the same in spirit as that which science teaches in thought; and the ethical neutrality by which its victories have been achieved is the outcome of that submission.

The good which it concerns us to remember is the good which it lies in our power to create—the good in our own lives and in our attitude towards the world. Insistence on belief in an external realisation of the good is a form of self-assertion, which, while it cannot secure the external good which it desires, can seriously impair the inward good which lies within our power, and destroy that reverence towards fact which constitutes both what is valuable in humility and what is fruitful in the scientific temper.

Human beings cannot, of course, wholly transcend human nature; something subjective, if only the interest that determines the direction of our attention, must remain in all our thought. But scientific philosophy comes nearer to objectivity than any other human pursuit, and gives us, therefore, the closest constant and the most intimate relation with the outer world that it is possible to achieve. To the primitive mind, everything is either friendly or hostile; but experience has shown that friendliness and hostility are not the conceptions by which the world is to be understood. Scientific philosophy thus represents, though as yet only in a nascent condition, a higher form of thought than any pre-scientific belief or imagination, and, like every approach to self-transcendence, it brings with it a rich reward in increase of scope and breadth and comprehension. Evolutionism, in spite of its appeals to particular scientific facts, fails to be a truly scientific philosophy because of its slavery to time, its ethical preoccupations, and its predominant interest in our mundane concerns and destiny. A truly scientific philosophy will be more humble, more piecemeal, more arduous, offering less glitter of outward mirage to flatter fallacious hopes, but more indifferent to fate, and more capable of accepting the world without the tyrannous imposition of our human and temporary demands.

Footnotes

[1] All the above quotations are from Burnet's *Early Greek Philosophy*, (2nd ed., 1908), pp. 146-156.

[2] *Republic*, 514, translated by Davies and Vaughan.

[3] This section, and also one or two pages in later sections, have been printed in a course of Lowell lectures *On our knowledge of the external world*, published by the Open Court Publishing Company. But I have left them here, as this is the context for which they were originally written.

[4] *Introduction to Metaphysics*, p. 1.

[5] Whinfield's translation of the *Masnavi* (Trübner, 1887), p. 34.

[6] *Ethics*, Bk. IV, Prop. LXII.

[7] Ib., Pt. IV, Df. I.

[8] *Ethics.* Pt. II. Df. VI.

<
div class="footnote">
1 2 3 4 5 6

1.
2.
3.
4.
5.
6.

Chapter 2

The Place of Science in a Liberal Education

I.

Science, to the ordinary reader of newspapers, is represented by a varying selection of sensational triumphs, such as wireless telegraphy and aeroplanes radio-activity and the marvels of modern alchemy. It is not of this aspect of science that I wish to speak. Science, in this aspect, consists of detached up-to-date fragments, interesting only until they are replaced by something newer and more up-to-date, displaying nothing of the systems of patiently constructed knowledge out of which, almost as a casual incident, have come the practically useful results which interest the man in the street. The increased command over the forces of nature which is derived from science is undoubtedly an amply sufficient reason for encouraging scientific research, but this reason has been so often urged and is so easily appreciated that other reasons, to my mind quite as important, are apt to be overlooked. It is with these other reasons, especially with the intrinsic value of a scientific habit of mind in forming our outlook on the world, that I shall be concerned in what follows.

The instance of wireless telegraphy will serve to illustrate the difference between the two points of view. Almost all the serious intellectual labour required for the possibility of this invention is due to three men—Faraday, Maxwell, and Hertz. In alternating layers of experiment and theory these three men built up the modern theory of electromagnetism, and demonstrated the identity of light with electromagnetic waves. The system which they discovered is one of profound intellectual interest, bringing together and unifying an endless variety of apparently detached phenomena, and displaying a cumulative mental power which cannot but afford delight to every generous spirit. The mechanical details which remained to be adjusted in order to utilise their discoveries for a practical system of telegraphy demanded, no doubt, very considerable ingenuity, but had not that broad sweep and that universality which could give them intrinsic interest as an object of disinterested contemplation.

From the point of view of training the mind, of giving that well-informed, impersonal outlook which constitutes culture in the good sense of this much-misused word, it seems to be generally held indisputable that a literary education is superior to one based on science. Even the warmest advocates of science are apt to rest their claims on the contention that culture ought to be sacrificed to utility. Those men of science who respect culture, when they associate with men learned in the classics, are apt to admit, not merely politely, but sincerely, a certain inferiority on their side, compensated doubtless by the services which science renders to humanity, but none the less real. And so long as this attitude exists among men of science, it tends to verify itself: the intrinsically valuable aspects of science tend to be sacrificed to the merely useful, and little attempt is made to preserve that leisurely, systematic survey by which the finer quality of mind is formed and nourished.

But even if there be, in present fact, any such inferiority as is supposed in the educational value of science, this is, I believe, not the fault of science itself, but the fault of the spirit in which science is taught. If its full possibilities were realised by those who teach it, I believe that its capacity of producing those habits of mind which constitute the highest mental excellence would be at least as great as that of literature, and more particularly of Greek and Latin literature. In saying this I have no wish whatever to disparage a classical education. I have not myself enjoyed its benefits, and my knowledge of Greek and Latin authors is derived almost wholly from translations. But I am firmly persuaded that the Greeks fully deserve all the admiration that is bestowed upon them, and that it is a very great and serious loss to be unacquainted with their writings. It is not by attacking them, but by drawing attention to neglected excellences in science, that I wish to conduct my argument.

One defect, however, does seem inherent in a purely classical education—namely, a too exclusive emphasis on the past. By

the study of what is absolutely ended and can never be renewed, a habit of criticism towards the present and the future is engendered. The qualities in which the present excels are qualities to which the study of the past does not direct attention, and to which, therefore, the student of Greek civilisation may easily become blind. In what is new and growing there is apt to be something crude, insolent, even a little vulgar, which is shocking to the man of sensitive taste; quivering from the rough contact, he retires to the trim gardens of a polished past, forgetting that they were reclaimed from the wilderness by men as rough and earth-soiled as those from whom he shrinks in his own day. The habit of being unable to recognise merit until it is dead is too apt to be the result of a purely bookish life, and a culture based wholly on the past will seldom be able to pierce through everyday surroundings to the essential splendour of contemporary things, or to the hope of still greater splendour in the future.
<

div class="poem">
"My eyes saw not the men of old;
And now their age away has rolled.
I weep—to think I shall not see
The heroes of posterity."

So says the Chinese poet; but such impartiality is rare in the more pugnacious atmosphere of the West, where the champions of past and future fight a never-ending battle, instead of combining to seek out the merits of both.

This consideration, which militates not only against the exclusive study of the classics, but against every form of culture which has become static, traditional, and academic, leads inevitably to the fundamental question: What is the true end of education? But before attempting to answer this question it will be well to define the sense in which we are to use the word "education." For this purpose I shall distinguish the sense in which I mean to use it from two others, both perfectly legitimate, the one broader and the other narrower than the sense in which I mean to use the word.

In the broader sense, education will include not only what we learn through instruction, but all that we learn through personal experience—the formation of character through the education of life. Of this aspect of education, vitally important as it is, I will say nothing, since its consideration would introduce topics quite foreign to the question with which we are concerned.

In the narrower sense, education may be confined to instruction, the imparting of definite information on various subjects, because such information, in and for itself, is useful in daily life. Elementary education—reading, writing, and arithmetic—is almost wholly of this kind. But instruction, necessary as it is, does not *per se* constitute education in the sense in which I wish to consider it.

Education, in the sense in which I mean it, may be defined as *the formation, by means of instruction, of certain mental habits and a certain outlook on life and the world*. It remains to ask ourselves, what mental habits, and what sort of outlook, can be hoped for as the result of instruction? When we have answered this question we can attempt to decide what science has to contribute to the formation of the habits and outlook which we desire.

Our whole life is built about a certain number—not a very small number—of primary instincts and impulses. Only what is in some way connected with these instincts and impulses appears to us desirable or important; there is no faculty, whether "reason" or "virtue" or whatever it may be called, that can take our active life and our hopes and fears outside the region controlled by these first movers of all desire. Each of them is like a queen-bee, aided by a hive of workers gathering honey; but when the queen is gone the workers languish and die, and the cells remain empty of their expected sweetness. So with each primary impulse in civilised man: it is surrounded and protected by a busy swarm of attendant derivative desires, which store up in its service whatever honey the surrounding world affords. But if the queen-impulse dies, the death-dealing influence, though retarded a little by habit, spreads slowly through all the subsidiary impulses, and a whole tract of life becomes inexplicably colourless. What was formerly full of zest, and so obviously worth doing that it raised no questions, has now grown dreary and purposeless: with a sense of disillusion we inquire the meaning of life, and decide, perhaps, that all is vanity. The search for an outside meaning that can *compel* an inner response must always be disappointed: all "meaning" must be at bottom related to our primary desires, and when they are extinct no miracle can restore to the world the value which they reflected upon it.

The purpose of education, therefore, cannot be to create any primary impulse which is lacking in the uneducated; the purpose can only be to enlarge the scope of those that human nature provides, by increasing the number and variety of attendant thoughts, and by showing where the most permanent satisfaction is to be found. Under the impulse of a Calvinistic horror of the "natural man," this obvious truth has been too often misconceived in the training of the young; "nature" has been falsely regarded as excluding all that is best in what is natural, and the endeavour to teach virtue has led to the production of stunted and contorted hypocrites instead of full-grown human beings. From such mistakes in education a better psychology or a kinder heart is beginning to preserve the present generation; we need, therefore, waste no more words on the theory that the purpose of education is to thwart or eradicate nature.

But although nature must supply the initial force of desire, nature is not, in the civilised man, the spasmodic, fragmentary, and yet violent set of impulses that it is in the savage. Each impulse has its constitutional ministry of thought and knowledge and reflection, through which possible conflicts of impulses are foreseen, and temporary impulses are controlled by the unifying impulse which may be called wisdom. In this way education destroys the crudity of instinct, and increases through knowledge the wealth and variety of the individual's contacts with the outside world, making him no longer an isolated fighting unit, but a citizen of the universe, embracing distant countries, remote regions of space, and vast stretches of past and future within the circle of his interests. It is this simultaneous softening in the insistence of desire and enlargement of its scope that is the chief moral end of education.

Closely connected with this moral end is the more purely intellectual aim of education, the endeavour to make us see and imagine the world in an objective manner, as far as possible as it is in itself, and not merely through the distorting medium of personal desire. The complete attainment of such an objective view is no doubt an ideal, indefinitely approachable, but not actually and fully realisable. Education, considered as a process of forming our mental habits and our outlook on the world, is to be judged successful in proportion as its outcome approximates to this ideal; in proportion, that is to say, as it gives us a true view of our place in society, of the relation of the whole human society to its non-human environment, and of the nature of the non-human world as it is in itself apart from our desires and interests. If this standard is admitted, we can return to the consideration of science, inquiring how far science contributes to such an aim, and whether it is in any respect superior to its rivals in educational practice.

II.

Two opposite and at first sight conflicting merits belong to science as against literature and art. The one, which is not inherently necessary, but is certainly true at the present day, is hopefulness as to the future of human achievement, and in particular as to the useful work that may be accomplished by any intelligent student. This merit and the cheerful outlook which it engenders prevent what might otherwise be the depressing effect of another aspect of science, to my mind also a merit, and perhaps its greatest merit—I mean the irrelevance of human passions and of the whole subjective apparatus where scientific truth is concerned. Each of these reasons for preferring the study of science requires some amplification. Let us begin with the first.

In the study of literature or art our attention is perpetually riveted upon the past: the men of Greece or of the Renaissance did better than any men do now; the triumphs of former ages, so far from facilitating fresh triumphs in our own age, actually increase the difficulty of fresh triumphs by rendering originality harder of attainment; not only is artistic achievement not cumulative, but it seems even to depend upon a certain freshness and *naïveté* of impulse and vision which civilisation tends to destroy. Hence comes, to those who have been nourished on the literary and artistic productions of former ages, a certain peevishness and undue fastidiousness towards the present, from which there seems no escape except into the deliberate vandalism which ignores tradition and in the search after originality achieves only the eccentric. But in such vandalism there is none of the simplicity and spontaneity out of which great art springs: theory is still the canker in its core, and insincerity destroys the advantages of a merely pretended ignorance.

The despair thus arising from an education which suggests no pre-eminent mental activity except that of artistic creation is wholly absent from an education which gives the knowledge of scientific method. The discovery of scientific method, except in pure mathematics, is a thing of yesterday; speaking broadly, we may say that it dates from Galileo. Yet already it has transformed the world, and its success proceeds with ever-accelerating velocity. In science men have discovered an activity of the very highest value in which they are no longer, as in art, dependent for progress upon the appearance of continually greater genius, for in science the successors stand upon the shoulders of their predecessors; where one man of supreme genius has invented a method, a thousand lesser men can apply it. No transcendent ability is required in order to make useful discoveries in science; the edifice of science needs its masons, bricklayers, and common labourers as well as its foremen, master-builders, and architects. In art nothing worth doing can be done without genius; in science even a very moderate capacity can contribute to a supreme achievement.

In science the man of real genius is the man who invents a new method. The notable discoveries are often made by his successors, who can apply the method with fresh vigour, unimpaired by the previous labour of perfecting it; but the mental calibre of the thought required for their work, however brilliant, is not so great as that required by the first inventor of the method. There are in science immense numbers of different methods, appropriate to different classes of problems; but over and above them all, there is something not easily definable, which may be called *the* method of science. It was formerly customary to identify this with the inductive method, and to associate it with the name of Bacon. But the true inductive method was not discovered by Bacon, and the true method of science is something which includes deduction as much as induction, logic and mathematics as much as botany and geology. I shall not attempt the difficult task of stating what the scientific method is, but I will try to indicate the temper of mind out of which the scientific method grows, which is the second of the two merits that were mentioned above as belonging to a scientific education.

The kernel of the scientific outlook is a thing so simple, so obvious, so seemingly trivial, that the mention of it may almost excite derision. The kernel of the scientific outlook is the refusal to regard our own desires, tastes, and interests as affording a key to the understanding of the world. Stated thus baldly, this may seem no more than a trite truism. But to remember it consistently in matters arousing our passionate partisanship is by no means easy, especially where the available evidence is uncertain and inconclusive. A few illustrations will make this clear.

Aristotle, I understand, considered that the stars must move in circles because the circle is the most perfect curve. In the absence of evidence to the contrary, he allowed himself to decide a question of fact by an appeal to æsthetico-moral considerations. In such a case it is at once obvious to us that this appeal was unjustifiable. We know now how to ascertain as a fact the way in which the heavenly bodies move, and we know that they do not move in circles, or even in accurate ellipses, or in any other kind of simply describable curve. This may be painful to a certain hankering after simplicity of pattern in the universe, but we know that in astronomy such feelings are irrelevant. Easy as this knowledge seems now, we owe it to the courage and insight of the first inventors of scientific method, and more especially of Galileo.

We may take as another illustration Malthus's doctrine of population. This illustration is all the better for the fact that his actual doctrine is now known to be largely erroneous. It is not his conclusions that are valuable, but the temper and method of his inquiry. As everyone knows, it was to him that Darwin owed an essential part of his theory of natural selection, and this was only possible because Malthus's outlook was truly scientific. His great merit lies in considering man not as the object of praise or blame, but as a part of nature, a thing with a certain characteristic behaviour from which certain consequences must follow. If the behaviour is not quite what Malthus supposed, if the consequences are not quite what he inferred, that may falsify his conclusions, but does not impair the value of his method. The objections which were made when his doctrine was new—that it was horrible and depressing, that people ought not to act as he said they did, and so on—were all such as implied an unscientific attitude of mind; as against all of them, his calm determination to treat man as a natural phenomenon marks an important advance over the reformers of the eighteenth century and the Revolution.

Under the influence of Darwinism the scientific attitude towards man has now become fairly common, and is to some people quite natural, though to most it is still a difficult and artificial intellectual contortion. There is however, one study which is as yet almost wholly untouched by the scientific spir-it—I mean the study of philosophy. Philosophers and the public imagine that the scientific spirit must pervade pages that bristle with allusions to ions, germ-plasms, and the eyes of shell-fish. But as the devil can quote Scripture, so the philo-sopher can quote science. The scientific spirit is not an affair of quotation, of externally acquired information, any more than manners are an affair of the etiquette-book. The scientific atti-tude of mind involves a sweeping away of all other desires in the interests of the desire to know—it involves suppression of hopes and fears, loves and hates, and the whole subjective emotional life, until we become subdued to the material, able to see it frankly, without preconceptions, without bias, without any wish except to see it as it is, and without any belief that what it is must be determined by some relation, positive or negative, to what we should like it to be, or to what we can easily imagine it to be.

Now in philosophy this attitude of mind has not as yet been achieved. A certain self-absorption, not personal, but human, has marked almost all attempts to conceive the universe as a whole. Mind, or some aspect of it—thought or will or sen-tience—has been regarded as the pattern after which the uni-verse is to be conceived, for no better reason, at bottom, than that such a universe would not seem strange, and would give us the cosy feeling that every place is like home. To conceive the universe as essentially progressive or essentially deterior-ating, for example, is to give to our hopes and fears a cosmic importance which *may*, of course, be justified, but which we have as yet no reason to suppose justified. Until we have learnt to think of it in ethically neutral terms, we have not arrived at a scientific attitude in philosophy; and until we have arrived at such an attitude, it is hardly to be hoped that philosophy will achieve any solid results.

I have spoken so far largely of the negative aspect of the sci-entific spirit, but it is from the positive aspect that its value is derived. The instinct of constructiveness, which is one of the chief incentives to artistic creation, can find in scientific sys-tems a satisfaction more massive than any epic poem. Disinter-ested curiosity, which is the source of almost all intellectual ef-fort, finds with astonished delight that science can unveil secrets which might well have seemed for ever undiscoverable. The desire for a larger life and wider interests, for an escape from private circumstances, and even from the whole recurring human cycle of birth and death, is fulfilled by the impersonal cosmic outlook of science as by nothing else. To all these must be added, as contributing to the happiness of the man of science, the admiration of splendid achievement, and the consciousness of inestimable utility to the human race. A life devoted to science is therefore a happy life, and its happiness is derived from the very best sources that are open to dwellers on this troubled and passionate planet.

Chapter 3

A Free Man's Worship

[Reprinted from the *Independent Review*, December, 1903.]
To Dr. Faustus in his study Mephistopheles told the history of the Creation, saying:

"The endless praises of the choirs of angels had begun to grow wearisome; for, after all, did he not deserve their praise? Had he not given them endless joy? Would it not be more amusing to obtain undeserved praise, to be worshipped by beings whom he tortured? He smiled inwardly, and resolved that the great drama should be performed.

"For countless ages the hot nebula whirled aimlessly through space. At length it began to take shape, the central mass threw off planets, the planets cooled, boiling seas and burning mountains heaved and tossed, from black masses of cloud hot sheets of rain deluged the barely solid crust. And now the first germ of life grew in the depths of the ocean, and developed rapidly in the fructifying warmth into vast forest trees, huge ferns springing from the damp mould, sea monsters breeding, fighting, devouring, and passing away. And from the monsters, as the play unfolded itself, Man was born, with the power of thought, the knowledge of good and evil, and the cruel thirst for worship. And Man saw that all is passing in this mad, monstrous world, that all is struggling to snatch, at any cost, a few brief moments of life before Death's inexorable decree. And Man said: 'There is a hidden purpose, could we but fathom it, and the purpose is good; for we must reverence something, and in the visible world there is nothing worthy of reverence.' And Man stood aside from the struggle, resolving that God intended harmony to come out of chaos by human efforts. And when he followed the instincts which God had transmitted to him from his ancestry of beasts of prey, he called it Sin, and asked God to forgive him. But he doubted whether he could be justly forgiven, until he invented a divine Plan by which God's wrath was to have been appeased. And seeing the present was bad, he made it yet worse, that thereby the future might be better. And he gave God thanks for the strength that enabled him to forgo even the joys that were possible. And God smiled; and when he saw that Man had become perfect in renunciation and worship, he sent another sun through the sky, which crashed into Man's sun; and all returned again to nebula.

"'Yes,' he murmured, 'it was a good play; I will have it performed again.'"

Such, in outline, but even more purposeless, more void of meaning, is the world which Science presents for our belief. Amid such a world, if anywhere, our ideals henceforward must find a home. That Man is the product of causes which had no prevision of the end they were achieving; that his origin, his growth, his hopes and fears, his loves and his beliefs, are but the outcome of accidental collocations of atoms; that no fire, no heroism, no intensity of thought and feeling, can preserve an individual life beyond the grave; that all the labours of the ages, all the devotion, all the inspiration, all the noonday brightness of human genius, are destined to extinction in the vast death of the solar system, and that the whole temple of Man's achievement must inevitably be buried beneath the débris of a universe in ruins—all these things, if not quite beyond dispute, are yet so nearly certain, that no philosophy which rejects them can hope to stand. Only within the scaffolding of these truths, only on the firm foundation of unyielding despair, can the soul's habitation henceforth be safely built.

How, in such an alien and inhuman world, can so powerless a creature as Man preserve his aspirations untarnished? A strange mystery it is that Nature, omnipotent but blind, in the revolutions of her secular hurryings through the abysses of space, has brought forth at last a child, subject still to her power, but gifted with sight, with knowledge of good and evil, with the capacity of judging all the works of his unthinking Mother. In spite of Death, the mark and seal of the parental control, Man is yet free, during his brief years, to examine, to criticise, to know, and in imagination to create. To him alone, in the world with which he is acquainted, this freedom belongs;

and in this lies his superiority to the resistless forces that control his outward life.

The savage, like ourselves, feels the oppression of his impotence before the powers of Nature; but having in himself nothing that he respects more than Power, he is willing to prostrate himself before his gods, without inquiring whether they are worthy of his worship. Pathetic and very terrible is the long history of cruelty and torture, of degradation and human sacrifice, endured in the hope of placating the jealous gods: surely, the trembling believer thinks, when what is most precious has been freely given, their lust for blood must be appeased, and more will not be required. The religion of Moloch—as such creeds may be generically called—is in essence the cringing submission of the slave, who dare not, even in his heart, allow the thought that his master deserves no adulation. Since the independence of ideals is not yet acknowledged, Power may be freely worshipped, and receive an unlimited respect, despite its wanton infliction of pain.

But gradually, as morality grows bolder, the claim of the ideal world begins to be felt; and worship, if it is not to cease, must be given to gods of another kind than those created by the savage. Some, though they feel the demands of the ideal, will still consciously reject them, still urging that naked Power is worthy of worship. Such is the attitude inculcated in God's answer to Job out of the whirlwind: the divine power and knowledge are paraded, but of the divine goodness there is no hint. Such also is the attitude of those who, in our own day, base their morality upon the struggle for survival, maintaining that the survivors are necessarily the fittest. But others, not content with an answer so repugnant to the moral sense, will adopt the position which we have become accustomed to regard as specially religious, maintaining that, in some hidden manner, the world of fact is really harmonious with the world of ideals. Thus Man creates God, all-powerful and all-good, the mystic unity of what is and what should be.

But the world of fact, after all, is not good; and, in submitting our judgment to it, there is an element of slavishness from which our thoughts must be purged. For in all things it is well to exalt the dignity of Man, by freeing him as far as possible from the tyranny of non-human Power. When we have realised that Power is largely bad, that man, with his knowledge of good and evil, is but a helpless atom in a world which has no such knowledge, the choice is again presented to us: Shall we worship Force, or shall we worship Goodness? Shall our God exist and be evil, or shall he be recognised as the creation of our own conscience?

The answer to this question is very momentous, and affects profoundly our whole morality. The worship of Force, to which Carlyle and Nietzsche and the creed of Militarism have accustomed us, is the result of failure to maintain our own ideals against a hostile universe: it is itself a prostrate submission to evil, a sacrifice of our best to Moloch. If strength indeed is to be respected, let us respect rather the strength of those who refuse that false "recognition of facts" which fails to recognise that facts are often bad. Let us admit that, in the world we know, there are many things that would be better otherwise, and that the ideals to which we do and must adhere are not realised in the realm of matter. Let us preserve our respect for truth, for beauty, for the ideal of perfection which life does not permit us to attain, though none of these things meet with the approval of the unconscious universe. If Power is bad, as it seems to be, let us reject it from our hearts. In this lies Man's true freedom: in determination to worship only the God created by our own love of the good, to respect only the heaven which inspires the insight of our best moments. In action, in desire, we must submit perpetually to the tyranny of outside forces; but in thought, in aspiration, we are free, free from our fellow-men, free from the petty planet on which our bodies impotently crawl, free even, while we live, from the tyranny of death. Let us learn, then, that energy of faith which enables us to live constantly in the vision of the good; and let us descend, in action, into the world of fact, with that vision always before us.

When first the opposition of fact and ideal grows fully visible, a spirit of fiery revolt, of fierce hatred of the gods, seems necessary to the assertion of freedom. To defy with Promethean constancy a hostile universe, to keep its evil always in view, always actively hated, to refuse no pain that the malice of Power can invent, appears to be the duty of all who will not bow before the inevitable. But indignation is still a bondage, for it compels our thoughts to be occupied with an evil world; and in the fierceness of desire from which rebellion springs there is a kind of self-assertion which it is necessary for the wise to overcome. Indignation is a submission of our thoughts, but not of our desires; the Stoic freedom in which wisdom consists is found in the submission of our desires, but not of our thoughts. From the submission of our desires springs the virtue of resignation; from the freedom of our thoughts springs the whole world of art and philosophy, and the vision of beauty by which, at last, we half reconquer the reluctant world. But the vision of beauty is possible only to unfettered contemplation, to thoughts not weighted by the load of eager wishes; and thus Freedom comes only to those who no longer ask of life that it shall yield them any of those personal goods that are subject to the mutations of Time.

Although the necessity of renunciation is evidence of the existence of evil, yet Christianity, in preaching it, has shown a wisdom exceeding that of the Promethean philosophy of rebellion. It must be admitted that, of the things we desire, some, though they prove impossible, are yet real goods; others, however, as ardently longed for, do not form part of a fully purified ideal. The belief that what must be renounced is bad, though sometimes false, is far less often false than untamed passion supposes; and the creed of religion, by providing a reason for proving that it is never false, has been the means of purifying our hopes by the discovery of many austere truths.

But there is in resignation a further good element: even real goods, when they are unattainable, ought not to be fretfully desired. To every man comes, sooner or later, the great renunciation. For the young, there is nothing unattainable; a good thing desired with the whole force of a passionate will, and yet impossible, is to them not credible. Yet, by death, by illness, by poverty, or by the voice of duty, we must learn, each one of us, that the world was not made for us, and that, however beautiful may be the things we crave, Fate may nevertheless forbid them. It is the part of courage, when misfortune comes, to bear without repining the ruin of our hopes, to turn away our thoughts from vain regrets. This degree of submission to Power is not only just and right: it is the very gate of wisdom.

But passive renunciation is not the whole of wisdom; for not by renunciation alone can we build a temple for the worship of our own ideals. Haunting foreshadowings of the temple appear in the realm of imagination, in music, in architecture, in the untroubled kingdom of reason, and in the golden sunset magic of lyrics, where beauty shines and glows, remote from the touch of sorrow, remote from the fear of change, remote from the failures and disenchantments of the world of fact. In the contemplation of these things the vision of heaven will shape itself in our hearts, giving at once a touchstone to judge the world about us, and an inspiration by which to fashion to our needs whatever is not incapable of serving as a stone in the sacred temple.

Except for those rare spirits that are born without sin, there is a cavern of darkness to be traversed before that temple can be entered. The gate of the cavern is despair, and its floor is paved with the gravestones of abandoned hopes. There Self must die; there the eagerness, the greed of untamed desire must be slain, for only so can the soul be freed from the empire of Fate. But out of the cavern the Gate of Renunciation leads again to the daylight of wisdom, by whose radiance a new insight, a new joy, a new tenderness, shine forth to gladden the pilgrim's heart.

When, without the bitterness of impotent rebellion, we have learnt both to resign ourselves to the outward rule of Fate and to recognise that the non-human world is unworthy of our worship, it becomes possible at last so to transform and refashion the unconscious universe, so to transmute it in the crucible of imagination, that a new image of shining gold replaces the old idol of clay. In all the multiform facts of the world—in the visual shapes of trees and mountains and clouds, in the events of the life of man, even in the very omnipotence of Death—the insight of creative idealism can find the reflection of a beauty which its own thoughts first made. In this way mind asserts its subtle mastery over the thoughtless forces of Nature. The more evil the material with which it deals, the more thwarting to untrained desire, the greater is its achievement in inducing the reluctant rock to yield up its hidden treasures, the prouder its victory in compelling the opposing forces to swell the pageant of its triumph. Of all the arts, Tragedy is the proudest, the most triumphant; for it builds its shining citadel in the very centre of the enemy's country, on the very summit of his highest mountain; from its impregnable watchtowers, his camps and arsenals, his columns and forts, are all revealed; within its walls the free life continues, while the legions of Death and Pain and Despair, and all the servile captains of tyrant Fate, afford the burghers of that dauntless city new spectacles of beauty. Happy those sacred ramparts, thrice happy the dwellers on that all-seeing eminence. Honour to those brave warriors who, through countless ages of warfare, have preserved for us the priceless heritage of liberty, and have kept undefiled by sacrilegious invaders the home of the unsubdued.

But the beauty of Tragedy does but make visible a quality which, in more or less obvious shapes, is present always and everywhere in life. In the spectacle of Death, in the endurance of intolerable pain, and in the irrevocableness of a vanished past, there is a sacredness, an overpowering awe, a feeling of the vastness, the depth, the inexhaustible mystery of existence, in which, as by some strange marriage of pain, the sufferer is bound to the world by bonds of sorrow. In these moments of insight, we lose all eagerness of temporary desire, all struggling and striving for petty ends, all care for the little trivial things that, to a superficial view, make up the common life of day by day; we see, surrounding the narrow raft illumined by the flickering light of human comradeship, the dark ocean on whose rolling waves we toss for a brief hour; from the great night without, a chill blast breaks in upon our refuge; all the loneliness of humanity amid hostile forces is concentrated upon the individual soul, which must struggle alone, with what of courage it can command, against the whole weight of a universe that cares nothing for its hopes and fears. Victory, in this struggle with the powers of darkness, is the true baptism into the glorious company of heroes, the true initiation into the overmastering beauty of human existence. From that awful encounter of the soul with the outer world, enunciation, wisdom, and charity are born; and with their birth a new life begins. To take into the inmost shrine of the soul the irresistible forces whose puppets we seem to be—Death and change, the irrevocableness of the past, and the powerlessness of man before the blind hurry of the universe from vanity to vanity—to feel these things and know them is to conquer them.

This is the reason why the Past has such magical power. The beauty of its motionless and silent pictures is like the enchanted purity of late autumn, when the leaves, though one breath would make them fall, still glow against the sky in golden glory. The Past does not change or strive; like Duncan, after life's fitful fever it sleeps well; what was eager and grasping, what was petty and transitory, has faded away, the things that were beautiful and eternal shine out of it like stars in the night. Its beauty, to a soul not worthy of it, is unendurable; but to a soul which has conquered Fate it is the key of religion.

The life of Man, viewed outwardly, is but a small thing in comparison with the forces of Nature. The slave is doomed to worship Time and Fate and Death, because they are greater than anything he finds in himself, and because all his thoughts are of things which they devour. But, great as they are, to think of them greatly, to feel their passionless splendour, is greater still. And such thought makes us free men; we no longer bow before the inevitable in Oriental subjection, but we absorb it, and make it a part of ourselves. To abandon the struggle for private happiness, to expel all eagerness of temporary desire, to burn with passion for eternal things—this is emancipation, and this is the free man's worship. And this liberation is effected by a contemplation of Fate; for Fate itself is subdued by the mind which leaves nothing to be purged by the purifying fire of Time.

United with his fellow-men by the strongest of all ties, the tie of a common doom, the free man finds that a new vision is with him always, shedding over every daily task the light of love. The life of Man is a long march through the night, surrounded by invisible foes, tortured by weariness and pain, towards a goal that few can hope to reach, and where none may tarry long. One by one, as they march, our comrades vanish from our sight, seized by the silent orders of omnipotent Death. Very brief is the time in which we can help them, in which their happiness or misery is decided. Be it ours to shed sunshine on their path, to lighten their sorrows by the balm of sympathy, to give them the pure joy of a never-tiring affection, to strengthen failing courage, to instil faith in hours of despair. Let us not weigh in grudging scales their merits and demerits, but let us think only of their need—of the sorrows, the difficulties, perhaps the blindnesses, that make the misery of their lives; let us remember that they are fellow-sufferers in the same darkness, actors in the same tragedy with ourselves. And so, when their day is over, when their good and their evil have become eternal by the immortality of the past, be it ours to feel that, where they suffered, where they failed, no deed of ours was the cause; but wherever a spark of the divine fire kindled in their hearts, we were ready with encouragement, with sympathy, with brave words in which high courage glowed.

Brief and powerless is Man's life; on him and all his race the slow, sure doom falls pitiless and dark. Blind to good and evil, reckless of destruction, omnipotent matter rolls on its relentless way; for Man, condemned to-day to lose his dearest, to-morrow himself to pass through the gate of darkness, it remains only to cherish, ere yet the blow falls, the lofty thoughts that ennoble his little day; disdaining the coward terrors of the slave of Fate, to worship at the shrine that his own hands have built; undismayed by the empire of chance, to preserve a mind free from the wanton tyranny that rules his outward life; proudly defiant of the irresistible forces that tolerate, for a moment, his knowledge and his condemnation, to sustain alone, a weary but unyielding Atlas, the world that his own ideals have fashioned despite the trampling march of unconscious power.

Chapter 4

The Study of Mathematics

In regard to every form of human activity it is necessary that the question should be asked from time to time, What is its purpose and ideal? In what way does it contribute to the beauty of human existence? As respects those pursuits which contribute only remotely, by providing the mechanism of life, it is well to be reminded that not the mere fact of living is to be desired, but the art of living in the contemplation of great things. Still more in regard to those avocations which have no end outside themselves, which are to be justified, if at all, as actually adding to the sum of the world's permanent possessions, it is necessary to keep alive a knowledge of their aims, a clear prefiguring vision of the temple in which creative imagination is to be embodied.

The fulfilment of this need, in what concerns the studies forming the material upon which custom has decided to train the youthful mind, is indeed sadly remote—so remote as to make the mere statement of such a claim appear preposterous. Great men, fully alive to the beauty of the contemplations to whose service their lives are devoted, desiring that others may share in their joys, persuade mankind to impart to the successive generations the mechanical knowledge without which it is impossible to cross the threshold. Dry pedants possess themselves of the privilege of instilling this knowledge: they forget that it is to serve but as a key to open the doors of the temple; though they spend their lives on the steps leading up to those sacred doors, they turn their backs upon the temple so resolutely that its very existence is forgotten, and the eager youth, who would press forward to be initiated to its domes and arches, is bidden to turn back and count the steps.

Mathematics, perhaps more even than the study of Greece and Rome, has suffered from this oblivion of its due place in civilisation. Although tradition has decreed that the great bulk of educated men shall know at least the elements of the subject, the reasons for which the tradition arose are forgotten, buried beneath a great rubbish-heap of pedantries and trivialities. To those who inquire as to the purpose of mathematics, the usual answer will be that it facilitates the making of machines, the travelling from place to place, and the victory over foreign nations, whether in war or commerce. If it be objected that these ends—all of which are of doubtful value—are not furthered by the merely elementary study imposed upon those who do not become expert mathematicians, the reply, it is true, will probably be that mathematics trains the reasoning faculties. Yet the very men who make this reply are, for the most part, unwilling to abandon the teaching of definite fallacies, known to be such, and instinctively rejected by the unsophisticated mind of every intelligent learner. And the reasoning faculty itself is generally conceived, by those who urge its cultivation, as merely a means for the avoidance of pitfalls and a help in the discovery of rules for the guidance of practical life. All these are undeniably important achievements to the credit of mathematics; yet it is none of these that entitles mathematics to a place in every liberal education. Plato, we know, regarded the contemplation of mathematical truths as worthy of the Deity; and Plato realised, more perhaps than any other single man, what those elements are in human life which merit a place in heaven. There is in mathematics, he says, "something which is *necessary* and cannot be set aside ... and, if I mistake not, of divine necessity; for as to the human necessities of which the Many talk in this connection, nothing can be more ridiculous than such an application of the words. *Cleinias.* And what are these necessities of knowledge, Stranger, which are divine and not human? *Athenian.* Those things without some use or knowledge of which a man cannot become a God to the world, nor a spirit, nor yet a hero, nor able earnestly to think and care for man" (*Laws*, p. 818).[10] Such was Plato's judgment of mathematics; but the mathematicians do not read Plato, while those who read him know no mathematics, and

53

regard his opinion upon this question as merely a curious aberration.

Mathematics, rightly viewed, possesses not only truth, but supreme beauty—a beauty cold and austere, like that of sculpture, without appeal to any part of our weaker nature, without the gorgeous trappings of painting or music, yet sublimely pure, and capable of a stern perfection such as only the greatest art can show. The true spirit of delight, the exaltation, the sense of being more than man, which is the touchstone of the highest excellence, is to be found in mathematics as surely as in poetry. What is best in mathematics deserves not merely to be learnt as a task, but to be assimilated as a part of daily thought, and brought again and again before the mind with ever-renewed encouragement. Real life is, to most men, a long second-best, a perpetual compromise between the ideal and the possible; but the world of pure reason knows no compromise, no practical limitations, no barrier to the creative activity embodying in splendid edifices the passionate aspiration after the perfect from which all great work springs. Remote from human passions, remote even from the pitiful facts of nature, the generations have gradually created an ordered cosmos, where pure thought can dwell as in its natural home, and where one, at least, of our nobler impulses can escape from the dreary exile of the actual world.

So little, however, have mathematicians aimed at beauty, that hardly anything in their work has had this conscious purpose. Much, owing to irrepressible instincts, which were better than avowed beliefs, has been moulded by an unconscious taste; but much also has been spoilt by false notions of what was fitting. The characteristic excellence of mathematics is only to be found where the reasoning is rigidly logical: the rules of logic are to mathematics what those of structure are to architecture. In the most beautiful work, a chain of argument is presented in which every link is important on its own account, in which there is an air of ease and lucidity throughout, and the premises achieve more than would have been thought possible, by means which appear natural and inevitable. Literature embodies what is general in particular circumstances whose universal significance shines through their individual dress; but mathematics endeavours to present whatever is most general in its purity, without any irrelevant trappings.

How should the teaching of mathematics be conducted so as to communicate to the learner as much as possible of this high ideal? Here experience must, in a great measure, be our guide; but some maxims may result from our consideration of the ultimate purpose to be achieved.

One of the chief ends served by mathematics, when rightly taught, is to awaken the learner's belief in reason, his confidence in the truth of what has been demonstrated, and in the value of demonstration. This purpose is not served by existing instruction; but it is easy to see ways in which it might be served. At present, in what concerns arithmetic, the boy or girl is given a set of rules, which present themselves as neither true nor false, but as merely the will of the teacher, the way in which, for some unfathomable reason, the teacher prefers to have the game played. To some degree, in a study of such definite practical utility, this is no doubt unavoidable; but as soon as possible, the reasons of rules should be set forth by whatever means most readily appeal to the childish mind. In geometry, instead of the tedious apparatus of fallacious proofs for obvious truisms which constitutes the beginning of Euclid, the learner should be allowed at first to assume the truth of everything obvious, and should be instructed in the demonstrations of theorems which are at once startling and easily verifiable by actual drawing, such as those in which it is shown that three or more lines meet in a point. In this way belief is generated; it is seen that reasoning may lead to startling conclusions, which nevertheless the facts will verify; and thus the instinctive distrust of whatever is abstract or rational is gradually overcome. Where theorems are difficult, they should be first taught as exercises in geometrical drawing, until the figure has become thoroughly familiar; it will then be an agreeable advance to be taught the logical connections of the various lines or circles that occur. It is desirable also that the figure illustrating a theorem should be drawn in all possible cases and shapes, that so the abstract relations with which geometry is concerned may of themselves emerge as the residue of similarity amid such great apparent diversity. In this way the abstract demonstrations should form but a small part of the instruction, and should be given when, by familiarity with concrete illustrations, they have come to be felt as the natural embodiment of visible fact. In this early stage proofs should not be given with pedantic fullness; definitely fallacious methods, such as that of superposition, should be rigidly excluded from the first, but where, without such methods, the proof would be very difficult, the result should be rendered acceptable by arguments and illustrations which are explicitly contrasted with demonstrations.

In the beginning of algebra, even the most intelligent child finds, as a rule, very great difficulty. The use of letters is a mystery, which seems to have no purpose except mystification. It is almost impossible, at first, not to think that every letter stands for some particular number, if only the teacher would reveal *what* number it stands for. The fact is, that in algebra the mind is first taught to consider general truths, truths which are not asserted to hold only of this or that particular thing, but of any one of a whole group of things. It is in the power of understanding and discovering such truths that the mastery of the intellect over the whole world of things actual and possible resides; and ability to deal with the general as such is one of the gifts that a mathematical education should bestow. But how little, as a rule, is the teacher of algebra able to explain the chasm which divides it from arithmetic, and how little is the learner assisted in his groping efforts at comprehension! Usually the method that has been adopted in arithmetic is continued: rules are set forth, with no adequate explanation of their grounds; the pupil learns to use the rules blindly, and presently, when he is able to obtain the answer that the teacher desires, he feels that he has mastered the difficulties of the subject. But of inner comprehension of the processes employed he has probably acquired almost nothing.

When algebra has been learnt, all goes smoothly until we reach those studies in which the notion of infinity is employed—the infinitesimal calculus and the whole of higher mathematics. The solution of the difficulties which formerly surrounded the mathematical infinite is probably the greatest achievement of which our own age has to boast. Since the beginnings of Greek thought these difficulties have been known; in every age the finest intellects have vainly endeavoured to answer the apparently unanswerable questions that had been asked by Zeno the Eleatic. At last Georg Cantor has found the answer, and has conquered for the intellect a new and vast province which had been given over to Chaos and old Night. It was assumed as self-evident, until Cantor and Dedekind established the opposite, that if, from any collection of things, some were taken away, the number of things left must always be less than the original number of things. This assumption, as a matter of fact, holds only of finite collections; and the rejection of it, where the infinite is concerned, has been shown to remove all the difficulties that had hitherto baffled human reason in this matter, and to render possible the creation of an exact science of the infinite. This stupendous fact ought to produce a revolution in the higher teaching of mathematics; it has itself added immeasurably to the educational value of the subject, and it has at last given the means of treating with logical precision many studies which, until lately, were wrapped in fallacy and obscurity. By those who were educated on the old lines, the new work is considered to be appallingly difficult, abstruse, and obscure; and it must be confessed that the discoverer, as is so often the case, has hardly himself emerged from the mists which the light of his intellect is dispelling. But inherently, the new doctrine of the infinite, to all candid and inquiring minds, has facilitated the mastery of higher mathematics; for hitherto, it has been necessary to learn, by a long process of sophistication, to give assent to arguments which, on first acquaintance, were rightly judged to be confused and erroneous. So far from producing a fearless belief in reason, a bold rejection of whatever failed to fulfil the strictest requirements of logic, a mathematical training, during the past two centuries, encouraged the belief that many things, which a rigid inquiry would reject as fallacious, must yet be accepted because they work in what the mathematician calls "practice." By this means, a timid, compromising spirit, or else a sacerdotal belief in mysteries not intelligible to the profane, has been bred where reason alone should have ruled. All this it is now time to sweep away; let those who wish to penetrate into the arcana of mathematics be taught at once the true theory in all its logical purity, and in the concatenation established by the very essence of the entities concerned.

If we are considering mathematics as an end in itself, and not as a technical training for engineers, it is very desirable to preserve the purity and strictness of its reasoning. Accordingly those who have attained a sufficient familiarity with its easier portions should be led backward from propositions to which they have assented as self-evident to more and more fundamental principles from which what had previously appeared as premises can be deduced. They should be taught—what the theory of infinity very aptly illustrates—that many propositions seem self-evident to the untrained mind which, nevertheless, a nearer scrutiny shows to be false. By this means they will be led to a sceptical inquiry into first principles, an examination of the foundations upon which the whole edifice of reasoning is built, or, to take perhaps a more fitting metaphor, the great trunk from which the spreading branches spring. At this stage, it is well to study afresh the elementary portions of mathematics, asking no longer merely whether a given proposition is true, but also how it grows out of the central principles of logic. Questions of this nature can now be answered with a precision and certainty which were formerly quite impossible; and in the chains of reasoning that the answer requires the unity of all mathematical studies at last unfolds itself.

In the great majority of mathematical text-books there is a total lack of unity in method and of systematic development of a central theme. Propositions of very diverse kinds are proved by whatever means are thought most easily intelligible, and much space is devoted to mere curiosities which in no way contribute to the main argument. But in the greatest works, unity and inevitability are felt as in the unfolding of a drama; in the premisses a subject is proposed for consideration, and in every subsequent step some definite advance is made towards mastery of its nature. The love of system, of interconnection, which is perhaps the inmost essence of the intellectual impulse, can find free play in mathematics as nowhere else. The learner who feels this impulse must not be repelled by an array of meaningless examples or distracted by amusing oddities, but must be encouraged to dwell upon central principles, to become familiar with the structure of the various subjects which are put before him, to travel easily over the steps of the more important deductions. In this way a good tone of mind is cultivated, and selective attention is taught to dwell by preference upon what is weighty and essential.

When the separate studies into which mathematics is divided have each been viewed as a logical whole, as a natural growth from the propositions which constitute their principles, the learner will be able to understand the fundamental science which unifies and systematises the whole of deductive reasoning. This is symbolic logic—a study which, though it owes its inception to Aristotle, is yet, in its wider developments, a product, almost wholly, of the nineteenth century, and is indeed, in the present day, still growing with great rapidity. The true method of discovery in symbolic logic, and probably also the best method for introducing the study to a learner acquainted with other parts of mathematics, is the analysis of actual examples of deductive reasoning, with a view to the discovery of the principles employed. These principles, for the most part, are so embedded in our ratiocinative instincts, that they are employed quite unconsciously, and can be dragged to light only by much patient effort. But when at last they have been found, they are seen to be few in number, and to be the sole source of everything in pure mathematics. The discovery that all mathematics follows inevitably from a small collection of fundamental laws is one which immeasurably enhances the intellectual beauty of the whole; to those who have been oppressed by the fragmentary and incomplete nature of most existing chains of deduction this discovery comes with all the overwhelming force of a revelation; like a palace emerging from the autumn mist as the traveller ascends an Italian hillside, the stately storeys of the mathematical edifice appear in their due order and proportion, with a new perfection in every part.

Until symbolic logic had acquired its present development, the principles upon which mathematics depends were always supposed to be philosophical, and discoverable only by the uncertain, unprogressive methods hitherto employed by philosophers. So long as this was thought, mathematics seemed to be not autonomous, but dependent upon a study which had quite other methods than its own. Moreover, since the nature of the postulates from which arithmetic, analysis, and geometry are to be deduced was wrapped in all the traditional obscurities of metaphysical discussion, the edifice built upon such dubious foundations began to be viewed as no better than a castle in the air. In this respect, the discovery that the true principles are as much a part of mathematics as any of their consequences has very greatly increased the intellectual satisfaction to be obtained. This satisfaction ought not to be refused to learners capable of enjoying it, for it is of a kind to increase our respect for human powers and our knowledge of the beauties belonging to the abstract world.

Philosophers have commonly held that the laws of logic, which underlie mathematics, are laws of thought, laws regulating the operations of our minds. By this opinion the true dignity of reason is very greatly lowered: it ceases to be an investigation into the very heart and immutable essence of all things actual and possible, becoming, instead, an inquiry into something more or less human and subject to our limitations. The contemplation of what is non-human, the discovery that our minds are capable of dealing with material not created by them, above all, the realisation that beauty belongs to the outer world as to the inner, are the chief means of overcoming the terrible sense of impotence, of weakness, of exile amid hostile powers, which is too apt to result from acknowledging the all-but omnipotence of alien forces. To reconcile us, by the exhibition of its awful beauty, to the reign of Fate—which is merely the literary personification of these forces—is the task of tragedy. But mathematics takes us still further from what is human, into the region of absolute necessity, to which not only the actual world, but every possible world, must conform; and even here it builds a habitation, or rather finds a habitation eternally standing, where our ideals are fully satisfied and our best hopes are not thwarted. It is only when we thoroughly understand the entire independence of ourselves, which belongs to this world that reason finds, that we can adequately realise the profound importance of its beauty.

Not only is mathematics independent of us and our thoughts, but in another sense we and the whole universe of existing things are independent of mathematics. The apprehension of this purely ideal character is indispensable, if we are to understand rightly the place of mathematics as one among the arts. It was formerly supposed that pure reason could decide, in some respects, as to the nature of the actual world: geometry, at least, was thought to deal with the space in which we live. But we now know that pure mathematics can never pronounce upon questions of actual existence: the world of reason, in a sense, controls the world of fact, but it is not at any point creative of fact, and in the application of its results to the world in time and space, its certainty and precision are lost among approximations and working hypotheses. The objects considered by mathematicians have, in the past, been mainly of a kind suggested by phenomena; but from such restrictions the abstract imagination should be wholly free. A reciprocal liberty must thus be accorded: reason cannot dictate to the world of facts, but the facts cannot restrict reason's privilege of dealing with whatever objects its love of beauty may cause to seem worthy of consideration. Here, as elsewhere, we build up our own ideals out of the fragments to be found in the world; and in the end it is hard to say whether the result is a creation or a discovery.

It is very desirable, in instruction, not merely to persuade the student of the accuracy of important theorems, but to persuade him in the way which itself has, of all possible ways, the most beauty. The true interest of a demonstration is not, as traditional modes of exposition suggest, concentrated wholly in the result; where this does occur, it must be viewed as a defect, to be remedied, if possible, by so generalising the steps of the proof that each becomes important in and for itself. An argument which serves only to prove a conclusion is like a story subordinated to some moral which it is meant to teach: for æsthetic perfection no part of the whole should be merely a means. A certain practical spirit, a desire for rapid progress, for conquest of new realms, is responsible for the undue emphasis upon results which prevails in mathematical instruction. The better way is to propose some theme for consideration—in geometry, a figure having important properties; in analysis, a function of which the study is illuminating, and so on. Whenever proofs depend upon some only of the marks by which we define the object to be studied, these marks should be isolated and investigated on their own account. For it is a defect, in an argument, to employ more premises than the conclusion demands: what mathematicians call elegance results from employing only the essential principles in virtue of which the thesis is true. It is a merit in Euclid that he advances as far as he is able to go without employing the axiom of parallels—not, as is often said, because this axiom is inherently objectionable, but because, in mathematics, every new axiom diminishes the generality of the resulting theorems, and the greatest possible generality is before all things to be sought.

Of the effects of mathematics outside its own sphere more has been written than on the subject of its own proper ideal. The effect upon philosophy has, in the past, been most notable, but most varied; in the seventeenth century, idealism and rationalism, in the eighteenth, materialism and sensationalism, seemed equally its offspring. Of the effect which it is likely to have in the future it would be very rash to say much; but in one respect a good result appears probable. Against that kind of scepticism which abandons the pursuit of ideals because the road is arduous and the goal not certainly attainable, mathematics, within its own sphere, is a complete answer. Too often it is said that there is no absolute truth, but only opinion and private judgment; that each of us is conditioned, in his view of the world, by his own peculiarities, his own taste and bias; that there is no external kingdom of truth to which, by patience and discipline, we may at last obtain admittance, but only truth for me, for you, for every separate person. By this habit of mind one of the chief ends of human effort is denied, and the supreme virtue of candour, of fearless acknowledgment of what is, disappears from our moral vision. Of such scepticism mathematics is a perpetual reproof; for its edifice of truths stands unshakable and inexpungable to all the weapons of doubting cynicism.

The effects of mathematics upon practical life, though they should not be regarded as the motive of our studies, may be used to answer a doubt to which the solitary student must always be liable. In a world so full of evil and suffering, retirement into the cloister of contemplation, to the enjoyment of delights which, however noble, must always be for the few only, cannot but appear as a somewhat selfish refusal to share the burden imposed upon others by accidents in which justice plays no part. Have any of us the right, we ask, to withdraw from present evils, to leave our fellow-men unaided, while we live a life which, though arduous and austere, is yet plainly good in its own nature? When these questions arise, the true answer is, no doubt, that some must keep alive the sacred fire, some must preserve, in every generation, the haunting vision which shadows forth the goal of so much striving. But when, as must sometimes occur, this answer seems too cold, when we are almost maddened by the spectacle of sorrows to which we bring no help, then we may reflect that indirectly the mathematician often does more for human happiness than any of his more practically active contemporaries. The history of science abundantly proves that a body of abstract propositions—even if, as in the case of conic sections, it remains two thousand years without effect upon daily life—may yet, at any moment, be used to cause a revolution in the habitual thoughts and occupations of every citizen. The use of steam and electricity—to take striking instances—is rendered possible only by mathematics. In the results of abstract thought the world possesses a capital of which the employment in enriching the common round has no hitherto discoverable limits. Nor does experience give any means of deciding what parts of mathematics will be found useful. Utility, therefore, can be only a consolation in moments of discouragement, not a guide in directing our studies.

For the health of the moral life, for ennobling the tone of an age or a nation, the austerer virtues have a strange power, exceeding the power of those not informed and purified by thought. Of these austerer virtues the love of truth is the chief, and in mathematics, more than elsewhere, the love of truth may find encouragement for waning faith. Every great study is not only an end in itself, but also a means of creating and sustaining a lofty habit of mind; and this purpose should be kept always in view throughout the teaching and learning of mathematics.

[10] This passage was pointed out to me by Professor Gilbert Murray.

Chapter 5

Mathematics and the Metaphysicians

The nineteenth century, which prided itself upon the invention of steam and evolution, might have derived a more legitimate title to fame from the discovery of pure mathematics. This science, like most others, was baptised long before it was born; and thus we find writers before the nineteenth century alluding to what they called pure mathematics. But if they had been asked what this subject was, they would only have been able to say that it consisted of Arithmetic, Algebra, Geometry, and so on. As to what these studies had in common, and as to what distinguished them from applied mathematics, our ancestors were completely in the dark.

Pure mathematics was discovered by Boole, in a work which he called the *Laws of Thought* (1854). This work abounds in asseverations that it is not mathematical, the fact being that Boole was too modest to suppose his book the first ever written on mathematics. He was also mistaken in supposing that he was dealing with the laws of thought: the question how people actually think was quite irrelevant to him, and if his book had really contained the laws of thought, it was curious that no one should ever have thought in such a way before. His book was in fact concerned with formal logic, and this is the same thing as mathematics.

Pure mathematics consists entirely of assertions to the effect that, if such and such a proposition is true of *anything*, then such and such another proposition is true of that thing. It is essential not to discuss whether the first proposition is really true, and not to mention what the anything is, of which it is supposed to be true. Both these points would belong to applied mathematics. We start, in pure mathematics, from certain rules of inference, by which we can infer that *if* one proposition is true, then so is some other proposition. These rules of inference constitute the major part of the principles of formal logic. We then take any hypothesis that seems amusing, and deduce its consequences. *If* our hypothesis is about *anything*, and not about some one or more particular things, then our deductions constitute mathematics. Thus mathematics may be defined as the subject in which we never know what we are talking about, nor whether what we are saying is true. People who have been puzzled by the beginnings of mathematics will, I hope, find comfort in this definition, and will probably agree that it is accurate.

As one of the chief triumphs of modern mathematics consists in having discovered what mathematics really is, a few more words on this subject may not be amiss. It is common to start any branch of mathematics—for instance, Geometry—with a certain number of primitive ideas, supposed incapable of definition, and a certain number of primitive propositions or axioms, supposed incapable of proof. Now the fact is that, though there are indefinables and indemonstrables in every branch of applied mathematics, there are none in pure mathematics except such as belong to general logic. Logic, broadly speaking, is distinguished by the fact that its propositions can be put into a form in which they apply to anything whatever. All pure mathematics—Arithmetic, Analysis, and Geometry—is built up by combinations of the primitive ideas of logic, and its propositions are deduced from the general axioms of logic, such as the syllogism and the other rules of inference. And this is no longer a dream or an aspiration. On the contrary, over the greater and more difficult part of the domain of mathematics, it has been already accomplished; in the few remaining cases, there is no special difficulty, and it is now being rapidly achieved. Philosophers have disputed for ages whether such deduction was possible; mathematicians have sat down and made the deduction. For the philosophers there is now nothing left but graceful acknowledgments.

The subject of formal logic, which has thus at last shown itself to be identical with mathematics, was, as every one knows, invented by Aristotle, and formed the chief study (other than theology) of the Middle Ages. But Aristotle never got beyond the syllogism, which is a very small part of the subject, and the schoolmen never got beyond Aristotle. If any proof were required of our superiority to the mediæval doctors, it might be found in this. Throughout the Middle Ages, almost all the best intellects devoted themselves to formal logic, whereas in the nineteenth century only an infinitesimal proportion of the world's thought went into this subject. Nevertheless, in each decade since 1850 more has been done to advance the subject than in the whole period from Aristotle to Leibniz. People have discovered how to make reasoning symbolic, as it is in Algebra, so that deductions are effected by mathematical rules. They have discovered many rules besides the syllogism, and a new branch of logic, called the Logic of Relatives,[11] has been invented to deal with topics that wholly surpassed the powers of the old logic, though they form the chief contents of mathematics.

It is not easy for the lay mind to realise the importance of symbolism in discussing the foundations of mathematics, and the explanation may perhaps seem strangely paradoxical. The fact is that symbolism is useful because it makes things difficult. (This is not true of the advanced parts of mathematics, but only of the beginnings.) What we wish to know is, what can be deduced from what. Now, in the beginnings, everything is self-evident; and it is very hard to see whether one self-evident proposition follows from another or not. Obviousness is always the enemy to correctness. Hence we invent some new and difficult symbolism, in which nothing seems obvious. Then we set up certain rules for operating on the symbols, and the whole thing becomes mechanical. In this way we find out what must be taken as premiss and what can be demonstrated or defined. For instance, the whole of Arithmetic and Algebra has been shown to require three indefinable notions and five indemonstrable propositions. But without a symbolism it would have been very hard to find this out. It is so obvious that two and two are four, that we can hardly make ourselves sufficiently sceptical to doubt whether it can be proved. And the same holds in other cases where self-evident things are to be proved.

But the proof of self-evident propositions may seem, to the uninitiated, a somewhat frivolous occupation. To this we might reply that it is often by no means self-evident that one obvious proposition follows from another obvious proposition; so that we are really discovering new truths when we prove what is evident by a method which is not evident. But a more interesting retort is, that since people have tried to prove obvious propositions, they have found that many of them are false. Self-evidence is often a mere will-o'-the-wisp, which is sure to lead us astray if we take it as our guide. For instance, nothing is plainer than that a whole always has more terms than a part, or that a number is increased by adding one to it. But these propositions are now known to be usually false. Most numbers are infinite, and if a number is infinite you may add ones to it as long as you like without disturbing it in the least. One of the merits of a proof is that it instils a certain doubt as to the result proved; and when what is obvious can be proved in some cases, but not in others, it becomes possible to suppose that in these other cases it is false.

The great master of the art of formal reasoning, among the men of our own day, is an Italian, Professor Peano, of the University of Turin.[12] He has reduced the greater part of mathematics (and he or his followers will, in time, have reduced the whole) to strict symbolic form, in which there are no words at all. In the ordinary mathematical books, there are no doubt fewer words than most readers would wish. Still, little phrases occur, such as *therefore, let us assume, consider*, or *hence it follows*. All these, however, are a concession, and are swept away by Professor Peano. For instance, if we wish to learn the whole of Arithmetic, Algebra, the Calculus, and indeed all that is usually called pure mathematics (except Geometry), we must start with a dictionary of three words. One symbol stands for *zero*, another for *number*, and a third for *next after*. What these ideas mean, it is necessary to know if you wish to become an arithmetician. But after symbols have been invented for these three ideas, not another word is required in the whole development. All future symbols are symbolically explained by means of these three. Even these three can be explained by means of the notions of *relation* and *class*; but this requires the Logic of Relations, which Professor Peano has never taken up. It must be admitted that what a mathematician has to know to begin with is not much. There are at most a dozen notions out of which all the notions in all pure mathematics (including Geometry) are compounded. Professor

Peano, who is assisted by a very able school of young Italian disciples, has shown how this may be done; and although the method which he has invented is capable of being carried a good deal further than he has carried it, the honour of the pioneer must belong to him.

Two hundred years ago, Leibniz foresaw the science which Peano has perfected, and endeavoured to create it. He was prevented from succeeding by respect for the authority of Aristotle, whom he could not believe guilty of definite, formal fallacies; but the subject which he desired to create now exists, in spite of the patronising contempt with which his schemes have been treated by all superior persons. From this "Universal Characteristic," as he called it, he hoped for a solution of all problems, and an end to all disputes. "If controversies were to arise," he says, "there would be no more need of disputation between two philosophers than between two accountants. For it would suffice to take their pens in their hands, to sit down to their desks, and to say to each other (with a friend as witness, if they liked), 'Let us calculate.'" This optimism has now appeared to be somewhat excessive; there still are problems whose solution is doubtful, and disputes which calculation cannot decide. But over an enormous field of what was formerly controversial, Leibniz's dream has become sober fact. In the whole philosophy of mathematics, which used to be at least as full of doubt as any other part of philosophy, order and certainty have replaced the confusion and hesitation which formerly reigned. Philosophers, of course, have not yet discovered this fact, and continue to write on such subjects in the old way. But mathematicians, at least in Italy, have now the power of treating the principles of mathematics in an exact and masterly manner, by means of which the certainty of mathematics extends also to mathematical philosophy. Hence many of the topics which used to be placed among the great mysteries—for example, the natures of infinity, of continuity, of space, time and motion—are now no longer in any degree open to doubt or discussion. Those who wish to know the nature of these things need only read the works of such men as Peano or Georg Cantor; they will there find exact and indubitable expositions of all these quondam mysteries.

In this capricious world, nothing is more capricious than posthumous fame. One of the most notable examples of posterity's lack of judgment is the Eleatic Zeno. This man, who may be regarded as the founder of the philosophy of infinity, appears in Plato's Parmenides in the privileged position of instructor to Socrates. He invented four arguments, all immeasurably subtle and profound, to prove that motion is impossible, that Achilles can never overtake the tortoise, and that an arrow in flight is really at rest. After being refuted by Aristotle, and by every subsequent philosopher from that day to our own, these arguments were reinstated, and made the basis of a mathematical renaissance, by a German professor, who probably never dreamed of any connection between himself and Zeno. Weierstrass,[13] by strictly banishing from mathematics the use of infinitesimals, has at last shown that we live in an unchanging world, and that the arrow in its flight is truly at rest. Zeno's only error lay in inferring (if he did infer) that, because there is no such thing as a state of change, therefore the world is in the same state at any one time as at any other. This is a consequence which by no means follows; and in this respect, the German mathematician is more constructive than the ingenious Greek. Weierstrass has been able, by embodying his views in mathematics, where familiarity with truth eliminates the vulgar prejudices of common sense, to invest Zeno's paradoxes with the respectable air of platitudes; and if the result is less delightful to the lover of reason than Zeno's bold defiance, it is at any rate more calculated to appease the mass of academic mankind.

Zeno was concerned, as a matter of fact, with three problems, each presented by motion, but each more abstract than motion, and capable of a purely arithmetical treatment. These are the problems of the infinitesimal, the infinite, and continuity. To state clearly the difficulties involved, was to accomplish perhaps the hardest part of the philosopher's task. This was done by Zeno. From him to our own day, the finest intellects of each generation in turn attacked the problems, but achieved, broadly speaking, nothing. In our own time, however, three men—Weierstrass, Dedekind, and Cantor—have not merely advanced the three problems, but have completely solved them. The solutions, for those acquainted with mathematics, are so clear as to leave no longer the slightest doubt or difficulty. This achievement is probably the greatest of which our age has to boast; and I know of no age (except perhaps the golden age of Greece) which has a more convincing proof to offer of the transcendent genius of its great men. Of the three problems, that of the infinitesimal was solved by Weierstrass; the solution of the other two was begun by Dedekind, and definitively accomplished by Cantor.

The infinitesimal played formerly a great part in mathematics. It was introduced by the Greeks, who regarded a circle as differing infinitesimally from a polygon with a very large number of very small equal sides. It gradually grew in importance, until, when Leibniz invented the Infinitesimal Calculus, it seemed to become the fundamental notion of all higher mathematics. Carlyle tells, in his *Frederick the Great*, how Leibniz used to discourse to Queen Sophia Charlotte of Prussia concerning the infinitely little, and how she would reply that on that subject she needed no instruction—the behaviour of courtiers had made her thoroughly familiar with it. But philosophers and mathematicians—who for the most part had less acquaintance with courts—continued to discuss this topic, though without making any advance. The Calculus required continuity, and continuity was supposed to require the infinitely little; but nobody could discover what the infinitely little might be. It was plainly not quite zero, because a sufficiently large number of infinitesimals, added together, were seen to make up a finite whole. But nobody could point out any fraction which was not zero, and yet not finite. Thus there was a deadlock. But at last Weierstrass discovered that the infinitesimal was not needed at all, and that everything could be accomplished without it. Thus there was no longer any need to suppose that there was such a thing. Nowadays, therefore, mathematicians are more dignified than Leibniz: instead of talking about the infinitely small, they talk about the infinitely great—a subject which, however appropriate to monarchs, seems, unfortunately, to interest them even less than the infinitely little interested the monarchs to whom Leibniz discoursed.

The banishment of the infinitesimal has all sorts of odd consequences, to which one has to become gradually accustomed. For example, there is no such thing as the next moment. The interval between one moment and the next would have to be infinitesimal, since, if we take two moments with a finite interval between them, there are always other moments in the interval. Thus if there are to be no infinitesimals, no two moments are quite consecutive, but there are always other moments between any two. Hence there must be an infinite number of moments between any two; because if there were a finite number one would be nearest the first of the two moments, and therefore next to it. This might be thought to be a difficulty; but, as a matter of fact, it is here that the philosophy of the infinite comes in, and makes all straight.

The same sort of thing happens in space. If any piece of matter be cut in two, and then each part be halved, and so on, the bits will become smaller and smaller, and can theoretically be made as small as we please. However small they may be, they can still be cut up and made smaller still. But they will always have *some* finite size, however small they may be. We never reach the infinitesimal in this way, and no finite number of divisions will bring us to points. Nevertheless there *are* points, only these are not to be reached by successive divisions. Here again, the philosophy of the infinite shows us how this is possible, and why points are not infinitesimal lengths.

As regards motion and change, we get similarly curious results. People used to think that when a thing changes, it must be in a state of change, and that when a thing moves, it is in a state of motion. This is now known to be a mistake. When a body moves, all that can be said is that it is in one place at one time and in another at another. We must not say that it will be in a neighbouring place at the next instant, since there is no next instant. Philosophers often tell us that when a body is in motion, it changes its position within the instant. To this view Zeno long ago made the fatal retort that every body always is where it is; but a retort so simple and brief was not of the kind to which philosophers are accustomed to give weight, and they have continued down to our own day to repeat the same phrases which roused the Eleatic's destructive ardour. It was only recently that it became possible to explain motion in detail in accordance with Zeno's platitude, and in opposition to the philosopher's paradox. We may now at last indulge the comfortable belief that a body in motion is just as truly where it is as a body at rest. Motion consists merely in the fact that bodies are sometimes in one place and sometimes in another, and that they are at intermediate places at intermediate times. Only those who have waded through the quagmire of philosophic speculation on this subject can realise what a liberation from antique prejudices is involved in this simple and straightforward commonplace.

The philosophy of the infinitesimal, as we have just seen, is mainly negative. People used to believe in it, and now they have found out their mistake. The philosophy of the infinite, on the other hand, is wholly positive. It was formerly supposed that infinite numbers, and the mathematical infinite generally, were self-contradictory. But as it was obvious that there were infinities—for example, the number of numbers—the contradictions of infinity seemed unavoidable, and philosophy seemed to have wandered into a "cul-de-sac." This difficulty led to Kant's antinomies, and hence, more or less indirectly, to much of Hegel's dialectic method. Almost all current philosophy is upset by the fact (of which very few philosophers are as yet aware) that all the ancient and respectable contradictions in the notion of the infinite have been once for all disposed of. The method by which this has been done is most interesting and instructive. In the first place, though people had talked glibly about infinity ever since the beginnings of Greek thought, nobody had ever thought of asking, What is infinity? If any philosopher had been asked for a definition of infinity, he might have produced some unintelligible rigmarole, but he would certainly not have been able to give a definition that had any meaning at all. Twenty years ago, roughly speaking, Dedekind and Cantor asked this question, and, what is more remarkable, they answered it. They found, that is to say, a perfectly precise definition of an infinite number or an infinite collection of things. This was the first and perhaps the greatest step. It then remained to examine the supposed contradictions in this notion. Here Cantor proceeded in the only proper way. He took pairs of contradictory propositions, in which both sides of the contradiction would be usually regarded as demonstrable, and he strictly examined the supposed proofs. He found that all proofs adverse to infinity involved a certain principle, at first sight obviously true, but destructive, in its consequences, of almost all mathematics. The proofs favourable to infinity, on the other hand, involved no principle that had evil consequences. It thus appeared that common sense had allowed itself to be taken in by a specious maxim, and that, when once this maxim was rejected, all went well.

The maxim in question is, that if one collection is part of another, the one which is a part has fewer terms than the one of which it is a part. This maxim is true of finite numbers. For example, Englishmen are only some among Europeans, and there are fewer Englishmen than Europeans. But when we come to infinite numbers, this is no longer true. This breakdown of the maxim gives us the precise definition of infinity. A collection of terms is infinite when it contains as parts other collections which have just as many terms as it has. If you can take away some of the terms of a collection, without diminishing the number of terms, then there are an infinite number of terms in the collection. For example, there are just as many even numbers as there are numbers altogether, since every number can be doubled. This may be seen by putting odd and even numbers together in one row, and even numbers alone in a row below:—
<
div class="block">
1, 2, 3, 4, 5, *ad infinitum.*
2, 4, 6, 8, 10, *ad infinitum.*
There are obviously just as many numbers in the row below as in the row above, because there is one below for each one above. This property, which was formerly thought to be a contradiction, is now transformed into a harmless definition of infinity, and shows, in the above case, that the number of finite numbers is infinite.

But the uninitiated may wonder how it is possible to deal with a number which cannot be counted. It is impossible to count up *all* the numbers, one by one, because, however many we may count, there are always more to follow. The fact is that counting is a very vulgar and elementary way of finding out how many terms there are in a collection. And in any case, counting gives us what mathematicians call the *ordinal* number of our terms; that is to say, it arranges our terms in an order or series, and its result tells us what type of series results from this arrangement. In other words, it is impossible to count things without counting some first and others afterwards, so that counting always has to do with order. Now when there are only a finite number of terms, we can count them in any order we like; but when there are an infinite number, what corresponds to counting will give us quite different results according to the way in which we carry out the operation. Thus the ordinal number, which results from what, in a general sense may be called counting, depends not only upon how many terms we have, but also (where the number of terms is infinite) upon the way in which the terms are arranged.

The fundamental infinite numbers are not ordinal, but are what is called *cardinal*. They are not obtained by putting our terms in order and counting them, but by a different method, which tells us, to begin with, whether two collections have the same number of terms, or, if not, which is the greater.[14] It does not tell us, in the way in which counting does, *what* number of terms a collection has; but if we define a number as the number of terms in such and such a collection, then this method enables us to discover whether some other collection that may be mentioned has more or fewer terms. An illustration will show how this is done. If there existed some country in which, for one reason or another, it was impossible to take a census, but in which it was known that every man had a wife and every woman a husband, then (provided polygamy was not a national institution) we should know, without counting, that there were exactly as many men as there were women in that country, neither more nor less. This method can be applied generally. If there is some relation which, like marriage, connects the things in one collection each with one of the things in another collection, and vice versa, then the two collections have the same number of terms. This was the way in which we found that there are as many even numbers as there are numbers. Every number can be doubled, and every even number can be halved, and each process gives just one number corresponding to the one that is doubled or halved. And in this way we can find any number of collections each of which has just as many terms as there are finite numbers. If every term of a collection can be hooked on to a number, and all the finite numbers are used once, and only once, in the process, then our collection must have just as many terms as there are finite numbers. This is the general method by which the numbers of infinite collections are defined.

But it must not be supposed that all infinite numbers are equal. On the contrary, there are infinitely more infinite numbers than finite ones. There are more ways of arranging the finite numbers in different types of series than there are finite numbers. There are probably more points in space and more moments in time than there are finite numbers. There are exactly as many fractions as whole numbers, although there are an infinite number of fractions between any two whole numbers. But there are more irrational numbers than there are whole numbers or fractions. There are probably exactly as many points in space as there are irrational numbers, and exactly as many points on a line a millionth of an inch long as in the whole of infinite space. There is a greatest of all infinite numbers, which is the number of things altogether, of every sort and kind. It is obvious that there cannot be a greater number than this, because, if everything has been taken, there is nothing left to add. Cantor has a proof that there is no greatest number, and if this proof were valid, the contradictions of infinity would reappear in a sublimated form. But in this one point, the master has been guilty of a very subtle fallacy, which I hope to explain in some future work.[15]

We can now understand why Zeno believed that Achilles cannot overtake the tortoise and why as a matter of fact he can overtake it. We shall see that all the people who disagreed with Zeno had no right to do so, because they all accepted premises from which his conclusion followed. The argument is this: Let Achilles and the tortoise start along a road at the same time, the tortoise (as is only fair) being allowed a handicap. Let Achilles go twice as fast as the tortoise, or ten times or a hundred times as fast. Then he will never reach the tortoise. For at every moment the tortoise is somewhere and Achilles is somewhere; and neither is ever twice in the same place while the race is going on. Thus the tortoise goes to just as many places as Achilles does, because each is in one place at one moment, and in another at any other moment. But if Achilles were to catch up with the tortoise, the places where the tortoise would have been would be only part of the places where Achilles would have been. Here, we must suppose, Zeno appealed to the maxim that the whole has more terms than the part.[16] Thus if Achilles were to overtake the tortoise, he would have been in more places than the tortoise; but we saw that he must, in any period, be in exactly as many places as the tortoise. Hence we infer that he can never catch the tortoise. This argument is strictly correct, if we allow the axiom that the whole has more terms than the part. As the conclusion is absurd, the axiom must be rejected, and then all goes well. But there is no good word to be said for the philosophers of the past two thousand years and more, who have all allowed the axiom and denied the conclusion.

The retention of this axiom leads to absolute contradictions, while its rejection leads only to oddities. Some of these oddities, it must be confessed, are very odd. One of them, which I call the paradox of Tristram Shandy, is the converse of the Achilles, and shows that the tortoise, if you give him time, will go just as far as Achilles. Tristram Shandy, as we know, employed two years in chronicling the first two days of his life, and lamented that, at this rate, material would accumulate faster than he could deal with it, so that, as years went by, he would be farther and farther from the end of his history. Now I maintain that, if he had lived for ever, and had not wearied of his task, then, even if his life had continued as event fully as it began, no part of his biography would have remained unwritten. For consider: the hundredth day will be described in the hundredth year, the thousandth in the thousandth year, and so on. Whatever day we may choose as so far on that he cannot hope to reach it, that day will be described in the corresponding year. Thus any day that may be mentioned will be written up sooner or later, and therefore no part of the biography will remain permanently unwritten. This paradoxical but perfectly true proposition depends upon the fact that the number of days in all time is no greater than the number of years.

Thus on the subject of infinity it is impossible to avoid conclusions which at first sight appear paradoxical, and this is the reason why so many philosophers have supposed that there were inherent contradictions in the infinite. But a little practice enables one to grasp the true principles of Cantor's doctrine, and to acquire new and better instincts as to the true and the false. The oddities then become no odder than the people at the antipodes, who used to be thought impossible because they would find it so inconvenient to stand on their heads.

The solution of the problems concerning infinity has enabled Cantor to solve also the problems of continuity. Of this, as of infinity, he has given a perfectly precise definition, and has shown that there are no contradictions in the notion so defined. But this subject is so technical that it is impossible to give any account of it here.

The notion of continuity depends upon that of *order*, since continuity is merely a particular type of order. Mathematics has, in modern times, brought order into greater and greater prominence. In former days, it was supposed (and philosophers are still apt to suppose) that quantity was the fundamental notion of mathematics. But nowadays, quantity is banished altogether, except from one little corner of Geometry, while order more and more reigns supreme. The investigation of different kinds of series and their relations is now a very large part of mathematics, and it has been found that this investigation can be conducted without any reference to quantity, and, for the most part, without any reference to number. All types of series are capable of formal definition, and their properties can be deduced from the principles of symbolic logic by means of the Algebra of Relatives. The notion of a limit, which is fundamental in the greater part of higher mathematics, used to be defined by means of quantity, as a term to which the terms of some series approximate as nearly as we please. But nowadays the limit is defined quite differently, and the series which it limits may not approximate to it at all. This improvement also is due to Cantor, and it is one which has revolutionised mathematics. Only order is now relevant to limits. Thus, for instance, the smallest of the infinite integers is the limit of the finite integers, though all finite integers are at an infinite distance from it. The study of different types of series is a general subject of which the study of ordinal numbers (mentioned above) is a special and very interesting branch. But the unavoidable technicalities of this subject render it impossible to explain to any but professed mathematicians.

Geometry, like Arithmetic, has been subsumed, in recent times, under the general study of order. It was formerly supposed that Geometry was the study of the nature of the space in which we live, and accordingly it was urged, by those who held that what exists can only be known empirically, that Geometry should really be regarded as belonging to applied mathematics. But it has gradually appeared, by the increase of non-Euclidean systems, that Geometry throws no more light upon the nature of space than Arithmetic throws upon the population of the United States. Geometry is a whole collection of deductive sciences based on a corresponding collection of sets of axioms. One set of axioms is Euclid's; other equally good sets of axioms lead to other results. Whether Euclid's axioms are true, is a question as to which the pure mathematician is indifferent; and, what is more, it is a question which it is theoretically impossible to answer with certainty in the affirmative. It might possibly be shown, by very careful measurements, that Euclid's axioms are false; but no measurements could ever assure us (owing to the errors of observation) that they are exactly true. Thus the geometer leaves to the man of science to decide, as best he may, what axioms are most nearly true in the actual world. The geometer takes any set of axioms that seem interesting, and deduces their consequences. What defines Geometry, in this sense, is that the axioms must give rise to a series of more than one dimension. And it is thus that Geometry becomes a department in the study of order.

In Geometry, as in other parts of mathematics, Peano and his disciples have done work of the very greatest merit as regards principles. Formerly, it was held by philosophers and mathematicians alike that the proofs in Geometry depended on the figure; nowadays, this is known to be false. In the best books there are no figures at all. The reasoning proceeds by the strict rules of formal logic from a set of axioms laid down to begin with. If a figure is used, all sorts of things seem obviously to follow, which no formal reasoning can prove from the explicit axioms, and which, as a matter of fact, are only accepted because they are obvious. By banishing the figure, it becomes possible to discover *all* the axioms that are needed; and in this way all sorts of possibilities, which would have otherwise remained undetected, are brought to light.

One great advance, from the point of view of correctness, has been made by introducing points as they are required, and not starting, as was formerly done, by assuming the whole of space. This method is due partly to Peano, partly to another Italian named Fano. To those unaccustomed to it, it has an air of somewhat wilful pedantry. In this way, we begin with the following axioms: (1) There is a class of entities called *points*. (2) There is at least one point. (3) If *a* be a point, there is at least one other point besides *a*. Then we bring in the straight line joining two points, and begin again with (4), namely, on the straight line joining *a* and *b*, there is at least one other point besides *a* and *b*. (5) There is at least one point not on the line *ab*. And so we go on, till we have the means of obtaining as many points as we require. But the word *space*, as Peano humorously remarks, is one for which Geometry has no use at all.

The rigid methods employed by modern geometers have deposed Euclid from his pinnacle of correctness. It was thought, until recent times, that, as Sir Henry Savile remarked in 1621, there were only two blemishes in Euclid, the theory of parallels and the theory of proportion. It is now known that these are almost the only points in which Euclid is free from blemish. Countless errors are involved in his first eight propositions. That is to say, not only is it doubtful whether his axioms are true, which is a comparatively trivial matter, but it is certain that his propositions do not follow from the axioms which he enunciates. A vastly greater number of axioms, which Euclid unconsciously employs, are required for the proof of his propositions. Even in the first proposition of all, where he constructs an equilateral triangle on a given base, he uses two circles which are assumed to intersect. But no explicit axiom assures us that they do so, and in some kinds of spaces they do not always intersect. It is quite doubtful whether our space belongs to one of these kinds or not. Thus Euclid fails entirely to prove his point in the very first proposition. As he is certainly not an easy author, and is terribly long-winded, he has no longer any but an historical interest. Under these circumstances, it is nothing less than a scandal that he should still be taught to boys in England.[17] A book should have either intelligibility or correctness; to combine the two is impossible, but to lack both is to be unworthy of such a place as Euclid has occupied in education.

The most remarkable result of modern methods in mathematics is the importance of symbolic logic and of rigid formalism.

Mathematicians, under the influence of Weierstrass, have shown in modern times a care for accuracy, and an aversion to slipshod reasoning, such as had not been known among them previously since the time of the Greeks. The great inventions of the seventeenth century—Analytical Geometry and the Infinitesimal Calculus—were so fruitful in new results that mathematicians had neither time nor inclination to examine their foundations. Philosophers, who should have taken up the task, had too little mathematical ability to invent the new branches of mathematics which have now been found necessary for any adequate discussion. Thus mathematicians were only awakened from their "dogmatic slumbers" when Weierstrass and his followers showed that many of their most cherished propositions are in general false. Macaulay, contrasting the certainty of mathematics with the uncertainty of philosophy, asks who ever heard of a reaction against Taylor's theorem? If he had lived now, he himself might have heard of such a reaction, for this is precisely one of the theorems which modern investigations have overthrown. Such rude shocks to mathematical faith have produced that love of formalism which appears, to those who are ignorant of its motive, to be mere outrageous pedantry.

The proof that all pure mathematics, including Geometry, is nothing but formal logic, is a fatal blow to the Kantian philosophy. Kant, rightly perceiving that Euclid's propositions could not be deduced from Euclid's axioms without the help of the figures, invented a theory of knowledge to account for this fact; and it accounted so successfully that, when the fact is shown to be a mere defect in Euclid, and not a result of the nature of geometrical reasoning, Kant's theory also has to be abandoned. The whole doctrine of *a priori* intuitions, by which Kant explained the possibility of pure mathematics, is wholly inapplicable to mathematics in its present form. The Aristotelian doctrines of the schoolmen come nearer in spirit to the doctrines which modern mathematics inspire; but the schoolmen were hampered by the fact that their formal logic was very defective, and that the philosophical logic based upon the syllogism showed a corresponding narrowness. What is now required is to give the greatest possible development to mathematical logic, to allow to the full the importance of relations, and then to found upon this secure basis a new philosophical logic, which may hope to borrow some of the exactitude and certainty of its mathematical foundation. If this can be successfully accomplished, there is every reason to hope that the near future will be as great an epoch in pure philosophy as the immediate past has been in the principles of mathematics. Great triumphs inspire great hopes; and pure thought may achieve, within our generation, such results as will place our time, in this respect, on a level with the greatest age of Greece.[18]

Footnotes

[11] This subject is due in the main to Mr. C.S. Peirce.

[12] I ought to have added Frege, but his writings were unknown to me when this article was written. [Note added in 1917.]

[13] Professor of Mathematics in the University of Berlin. He died in 1897.

[14] [Note added in 1917.] Although some infinite numbers are greater than some others, it cannot be proved that of any two infinite numbers one must be the greater.

[15] Cantor was not guilty of a fallacy on this point. His proof that there is no greatest number is valid. The solution of the puzzle is complicated and depends upon the theory of types, which is explained in *Principia Mathematica*, Vol. I (Camb. Univ. Press, 1910). [Note added in 1917.]

[16] This must not be regarded as a historically correct account of what Zeno actually had in mind. It is a new argument for his conclusion, not the argument which influenced him. On this point, see e.g. C.D. Broad, "Note on Achilles and the Tortoise," *Mind*, N.S., Vol. XXII, pp. 318-19. Much valuable work on the interpretation of Zeno has been done since this article was written. [Note added in 1917.]

[17] Since the above was written, he has ceased to be used as a textbook. But I fear many of the books now used are so bad that the change is no great improvement. [Note added in 1917.]

[18] The greatest age of Greece was brought to an end by the Peloponnesian War. [Note added in 1917.]

Chapter 6

On Scientific Method in Philosophy

When we try to ascertain the motives which have led men to the investigation of philosophical questions, we find that, broadly speaking, they can be divided into two groups, often antagonistic, and leading to very divergent systems. These two groups of motives are, on the one hand, those derived from religion and ethics, and, on the other hand, those derived from science. Plato, Spinoza, and Hegel may be taken as typical of the philosophers whose interests are mainly religious and ethical, while Leibniz, Locke, and Hume may be taken as representatives of the scientific wing. In Aristotle, Descartes, Berkeley, and Kant we find both groups of motives strongly present.

Herbert Spencer, in whose honour we are assembled to-day, would naturally be classed among scientific philosophers: it was mainly from science that he drew his data, his formulation of problems, and his conception of method. But his strong religious sense is obvious in much of his writing, and his ethical pre-occupations are what make him value the conception of evolution—that conception in which, as a whole generation has believed, science and morals are to be united in fruitful and indissoluble marriage.

It is my belief that the ethical and religious motives in spite of the splendidly imaginative systems to which they have given rise, have been on the whole a hindrance to the progress of philosophy, and ought now to be consciously thrust aside by those who wish to discover philosophical truth. Science, originally, was entangled in similar motives, and was thereby hindered in its advances. It is, I maintain, from science, rather than from ethics and religion, that philosophy should draw its inspiration.

But there are two different ways in which a philosophy may seek to base itself upon science. It may emphasise the most general *results* of science, and seek to give even greater generality and unity to these results. Or it may study the *methods* of science, and seek to apply these methods, with the necessary adaptations, to its own peculiar province. Much philosophy inspired by science has gone astray through preoccupation with the *results* momentarily supposed to have been achieved. It is not results, but *methods* that can be transferred with profit from the sphere of the special sciences to the sphere of philosophy. What I wish to bring to your notice is the possibility and importance of applying to philosophical problems certain broad principles of method which have been found successful in the study of scientific questions.

The opposition between a philosophy guided by scientific method and a philosophy dominated by religious and ethical ideas may be illustrated by two notions which are very prevalent in the works of philosophers, namely the notion of *the universe*, and the notion of *good and evil*. A philosopher is expected to tell us something about the nature of the universe as a whole, and to give grounds for either optimism or pessimism. Both these expectations seem to me mistaken. I believe the conception of "the universe" to be, as its etymology indicates, a mere relic of pre-Copernican astronomy: and I believe the question of optimism and pessimism to be one which the philosopher will regard as outside his scope, except, possibly, to the extent of maintaining that it is insoluble.

In the days before Copernicus, the conception of the "universe" was defensible on scientific grounds: the diurnal revolution of the heavenly bodies bound them together as all parts of one system, of which the earth was the centre. Round this apparent scientific fact, many human desires rallied: the wish to believe Man important in the scheme of things, the theoretical desire for a comprehensive understanding of the Whole, the hope that the course of nature might be guided by some sympathy with our wishes. In this way, an ethically inspired system of metaphysics grew up, whose anthropocentrism was apparently warranted by the geocentrism of astronomy. When Copernicus swept away the astronomical basis of this system of thought, it had grown so familiar, and had associated itself so intimately with men's aspirations, that it survived with scarcely diminished force—survived even Kant's "Copernican revolution," and is still now the unconscious premiss of most metaphysical systems.

The oneness of the world is an almost undiscussed postulate of most metaphysics. "Reality is not merely one and self-consistent, but is a system of reciprocally determinate parts"[19]—such a statement would pass almost unnoticed as a mere truism. Yet I believe that it embodies a failure to effect thoroughly the "Copernican revolution," and that the apparent oneness of the world is merely the oneness of what is seen by a single spectator or apprehended by a single mind. The Critical Philosophy, although it intended to emphasise the subjective element in many apparent characteristics of the world, yet, by regarding the world in itself as unknowable, so concentrated attention upon the subjective representation that its subjectivity was soon forgotten. Having recognised the categories as the work of the mind, it was paralysed by its own recognition, and abandoned in despair the attempt to undo the work of subjective falsification. In part, no doubt, its despair was well founded, but not, I think, in any absolute or ultimate sense. Still less was it a ground for rejoicing, or for supposing that the nescience to which it ought to have given rise could be legitimately exchanged for a metaphysical dogmatism.

I.

As regards our present question, namely, the question of the unity of the world, the right method, as I think, has been indicated by William James.[20] "Let us now turn our backs upon ineffable or unintelligible ways of accounting for the world's oneness, and inquire whether, instead of being a principle, the 'oneness' affirmed may not merely be a name like 'substance' descriptive of the fact that certain *specific and verifiable connections* are found among the parts of the experiential flux... . We can easily conceive of things that shall have no connection whatever with each other. We may assume them to inhabit different times and spaces, as the dreams of different persons do even now. They may be so unlike and incommensurable, and so inert towards one another, as never to jostle or interfere. Even now there may actually be whole universes so disparate from ours that we who know ours have no means of perceiving that they exist. We conceive their diversity, however; and by that fact the whole lot of them form what is known in logic as 'a universe of discourse.' To form a universe of discourse argues, as this example shows, no further kind of connexion. The importance attached by certain monistic writers to the fact that any chaos may become a universe by merely being named, is to me incomprehensible." We are thus left with two kinds of unity in the experienced world; the one what we may call the epistemological unity, due merely to the fact that my experienced world is what *one* experience selects from the sum total of existence: the other that tentative and partial unity exhibited in the prevalence of scientific laws in those portions of the world which science has hitherto mastered. Now a generalisation based upon either of these kinds of unity would be fallacious. That the things which we experience have the common property of being experienced by us is a truism from which obviously nothing of importance can be deducible: it is clearly fallacious to draw from the fact that whatever we experience is experienced the conclusion that therefore everything must be experienced. The generalisation of the second kind of unity, namely, that derived from scientific laws, would be equally fallacious, though the fallacy is a trifle less elementary. In order to explain it let us consider for a moment what is called the reign of law.

People often speak as though it were a remarkable fact that the physical world is subject to invariable laws. In fact, however, it is not easy to see how such a world could fail to obey general laws. Taking any arbitrary set of points in space, there is a function of the time corresponding to these points, i.e. expressing the motion of a particle which traverses these points: this function may be regarded as a general law to which the behaviour of such a particle is subject. Taking all such functions for all the particles in the universe, there will be theoretically some one formula embracing them all, and this formula may be regarded as the single and supreme law of the spatio-temporal world. Thus what is surprising in physics is not the existence of general laws, but their extreme simplicity. It is not the uniformity of nature that should surprise us, for, by sufficient analytic ingenuity, any conceivable course of nature might be shown to exhibit uniformity. What should surprise us is the fact that the uniformity is simple enough for us to be able to discover it. But it is just this characteristic of simplicity in the laws of nature hitherto discovered which it would be fallacious to generalise, for it is obvious that simplicity has been a part cause of their discovery, and can, therefore, give no ground for the supposition that other undiscovered laws are equally simple.

The fallacies to which these two kinds of unity have given rise suggest a caution as regards all use in philosophy of general *results* that science is supposed to have achieved. In the first place, in generalising these results beyond past experience, it is necessary to examine very carefully whether there is not some reason making it more probable that these results should hold of all that has been experienced than that they should hold of things universally. The sum total of what is experienced by mankind is a selection from the sum total of what exists, and any general character exhibited by this selection may be due to the manner of selecting rather than to the general character of that from which experience selects. In the second place, the most general results of science are the least certain and the most liable to be upset by subsequent research. In utilizing these results as the basis of a philosophy, we sacrifice the most valuable and remarkable characteristic of scientific method, namely, that, although almost everything in science is found sooner or later to require some correction, yet this correction is almost always such as to leave untouched, or only slightly modified, the greater part of the results which have been deduced from the premiss subsequently discovered to be faulty. The prudent man of science acquires a certain instinct as to the kind of uses which may be made of present scientific beliefs without incurring the danger of complete and utter refutation from the modifications likely to be introduced by subsequent discoveries. Unfortunately the use of scientific generalisations of a sweeping kind as the basis of philosophy is just that kind of use which an instinct of scientific caution would avoid, since, as a rule, it would only lead to true results if the generalisation upon which it is based stood in *no* need of correction.

We may illustrate these general considerations by means of two examples, namely, the conservation of energy and the principle of evolution.

(1) Let us begin with the conservation of energy, or, as Herbert Spencer used to call it, the persistence of force. He says:[21]
<
div class="block">
"Before taking a first step in the rational interpretation of Evolution, it is needful to recognise, not only the facts that Matter is indestructible and Motion continuous, but also the fact that Force persists. An attempt to assign the *causes* of Evolution would manifestly be absurd if that agency to which the metamorphosis in general and in detail is due, could either come into existence or cease to exist. The succession of phenomena would in such case be altogether arbitrary, and deductive Science impossible."

This paragraph illustrates the kind of way in which the philosopher is tempted to give an air of absoluteness and necessity to empirical generalisations, of which only the approximate truth in the regions hitherto investigated can be guaranteed by the unaided methods of science. It is very often said that the persistence of something or other is a necessary presupposition of all scientific investigation, and this presupposition is then thought to be exemplified in some quantity which physics declares to be constant. There are here, as it seems to me, three distinct errors. First, the detailed scientific investigation of nature does not *presuppose* any such general laws as its results are found to verify. Apart from particular observations, science need presuppose nothing except the general principles of logic, and these principles are not laws of nature, for they are merely hypothetical, and apply not only to the actual world but to whatever is *possible*. The second error consists in the identification of a constant quantity with a persistent entity. Energy is a certain function of a physical system, but is not a thing or substance persisting throughout the changes of the system. The same is true of mass, in spite of the fact that mass has often been defined as *quantity of matter*. The whole conception, of quantity, involving, as it does, numerical measurement based largely upon conventions, is far more artificial, far more an embodiment of mathematical convenience, than is commonly believed by those who philosophise on physics. Thus even if (which I cannot for a moment admit) the persistence of some entity were among the necessary postulates of science, it would be a sheer error to infer from this the constancy of any physical quantity, or the *a priori* necessity of any such constancy which may be empirically discovered. In the third place, it has become more and more evident with the progress of physics that large generalisations, such as the conservation of energy or mass, are far from certain and are very likely only approximate. Mass, which used to be regarded as the most indubitable of physical quantities, is now generally believed to vary according to velocity, and to be, in fact, a vector quantity which at a given moment is different in different directions. The detailed conclusions deduced from the supposed constancy of mass for such motions as used to be studied in physics will remain very nearly exact, and therefore over the field of the older investigations very little modification of the older results is required. But as soon as such a principle as the conservation of mass or of energy is erected into a universal *a priori* law, the slightest failure in absolute exactness is fatal, and the whole philosophic structure raised upon this foundation is necessarily ruined. The prudent philosopher, therefore, though he may with advantage study the methods of physics, will be very chary of basing anything upon what happen at the moment to be the most general results apparently obtained by those methods.

(2) The philosophy of evolution, which was to be our second example, illustrates the same tendency to hasty generalisation, and also another sort, namely, the undue preoccupation with ethical notions. There are two kinds of evolutionist philosophy, of which both Hegel and Spencer represent the older and less radical kind, while Pragmatism and Bergson represent the more modern and revolutionary variety. But both these sorts of evolutionism have in common the emphasis on *progress*, that is, upon a continual change from the worse to the better, or from the simpler to the more complex. It would be unfair to attribute to Hegel any scientific motive or foundation, but all the other evolutionists, including Hegel's modern disciples, have derived their impetus very largely from the history of biological development. To a philosophy which derives a law of universal progress from this history there are two objections. First, that this history itself is concerned with a very small selection of facts confined to an infinitesimal fragment of space and time, and even on scientific grounds probably not an average sample of events in the world at large. For we know that decay as well as growth is a normal occurrence in the world. An extra-terrestrial philosopher, who had watched a single youth up to the age of twenty-one and had never come across any other human being, might conclude that it is the nature of human beings to grow continually taller and wiser in an indefinite progress towards perfection; and this generalisation would be just as well founded as the generalisation which evolutionists base upon the previous history of this planet. Apart, however, from this scientific objection to evolutionism, there is another, derived from the undue admixture of ethical notions in the very idea of progress from which evolutionism derives its charm. Organic life, we are told, has developed gradually from the protozoon to the philosopher, and this development, we are assured, is indubitably an advance. Unfortunately it is the philosopher, not the protozoon, who gives us this assurance, and we can have no security that the impartial outsider would agree with the philosopher's self-complacent assumption. This point has been illustrated by the philosopher Chuang Tzŭ in the following instructive anecdote:

<
div class="block">
"The Grand Augur, in his ceremonial robes, approached the shambles and thus addressed the pigs: 'How can you object to die? I shall fatten you for three months. I shall discipline myself for ten days and fast for three. I shall strew fine grass, and place you bodily upon a carved sacrificial dish. Does not this satisfy you?'

Then, speaking from the pigs' point of view, he continued: 'It is better, perhaps, after all, to live on bran and escape the shambles... .'

'But then,' added he, speaking from his own point of view,' to enjoy honour when alive one would readily die on a war-shield or in the headsman's basket.'

So he rejected the pigs' point of view and adopted his own point of view. In what sense, then, was he different from the pigs?"

I much fear that the evolutionists too often resemble the Grand Augur and the pigs.

The ethical element which has been prominent in many of the most famous systems of philosophy is, in my opinion, one of the most serious obstacles to the victory of scientific method in the investigation of philosophical questions. Human ethical notions, as Chuang Tzǔ perceived, are essentially anthropocentric, and involve, when used in metaphysics, an attempt, however veiled, to legislate for the universe on the basis of the present desires of men. In this way they interfere with that receptivity to fact which is the essence of the scientific attitude towards the world. To regard ethical notions as a key to the understanding of the world is essentially pre-Copernican. It is to make man, with the hopes and ideals which he happens to have at the present moment, the centre of the universe and the interpreter of its supposed aims and purposes. Ethical metaphysics is fundamentally an attempt, however disguised, to give legislative force to our own wishes. This may, of course, be questioned, but I think that it is confirmed by a consideration of the way in which ethical notions arise. Ethics is essentially a product of the gregarious instinct, that is to say, of the instinct to co-operate with those who are to form our own group against those who belong to other groups. Those who belong to our own group are good; those who belong to hostile groups are wicked. The ends which are pursued by our own group are desirable ends, the ends pursued by hostile groups are nefarious. The subjectivity of this situation is not apparent to the gregarious animal, which feels that the general principles of justice are on the side of its own herd. When the animal has arrived at the dignity of the metaphysician, it invents ethics as the embodiment of its belief in the justice of its own herd. So the Grand Augur invokes ethics as the justification of Augurs in their conflicts with pigs. But, it may be said, this view of ethics takes no account of such truly ethical notions as that of self-sacrifice. This, however, would be a mistake. The success of gregarious animals in the struggle for existence depends upon co-operation within the herd, and co-operation requires sacrifice, to some extent, of what would otherwise be the interest of the individual. Hence arises a conflict of desires and instincts, since both self-preservation and the preservation of the herd are biological ends to the individual. Ethics is in origin the art of recommending to others the sacrifices required for co-operation with oneself. Hence, by reflexion, it comes, through the operation of social justice, to recommend sacrifices by oneself, but all ethics, however refined, remains more or less subjective. Even vegetarians do not hesitate, for example, to save the life of a man in a fever, although in doing so they destroy the lives of many millions of microbes. The view of the world taken by the philosophy derived from ethical notions is thus never impartial and therefore never fully scientific. As compared with science, it fails to achieve the imaginative liberation from self which is necessary to such understanding of the world as man can hope to achieve, and the philosophy which it inspires is always more or less parochial, more or less infected with the prejudices of a time and a place.

I do not deny the importance or value, within its own sphere, of the kind of philosophy which is inspired by ethical notions. The ethical work of Spinoza, for example, appears to me of the very highest significance, but what is valuable in such work is not any metaphysical theory as to the nature of the world to which it may give rise, nor indeed anything which can be proved or disproved by argument. What is valuable is the indication of some new way of feeling towards life and the world, some way of feeling by which our own existence can acquire more of the characteristics which we must deeply desire. The value of such work, however immeasurable it is, belongs with practice and not with theory. Such theoretic importance as it may possess is only in relation to human nature, not in relation to the world at large. The scientific philosophy, therefore, which aims only at understanding the world and not directly at any other improvement of human life, cannot take account of ethical notions without being turned aside from that submission to fact which is the essence of the scientific temper.

II.

If the notion of the universe and the notion of good and evil are extruded from scientific philosophy, it may be asked what specific problems remain for the philosopher as opposed to the man of science? It would be difficult to give a precise answer to this question, but certain characteristics may be noted as distinguishing the province of philosophy from that of the special sciences.

In the first place a philosophical proposition must be general. It must not deal specially with things on the surface of the earth, or with the solar system, or with any other portion of space and time. It is this need of generality which has led to the belief that philosophy deals with the universe as a whole. I do not believe that this belief is justified, but I do believe that a philosophical proposition must be applicable to everything that exists or may exist. It might be supposed that this admission would be scarcely distinguishable from the view which I wish to reject. This, however, would be an error, and an important one. The traditional view would make the universe itself the subject of various predicates which could not be applied to any particular thing in the universe, and the ascription of such peculiar predicates to the universe would be the special business of philosophy. I maintain, on the contrary, that there are no propositions of which the "universe" is the subject; in other words, that there is no such thing as the "universe." What I do maintain is that there are general propositions which may be asserted of each individual thing, such as the propositions of logic. This does not involve that all the things there are form a whole which could be regarded as another thing and be made the subject of predicates. It involves only the assertion that there are properties which belong to each separate thing, not that there are properties belonging to the whole of things collectively. The philosophy which I wish to advocate may be called logical atomism or absolute pluralism, because, while maintaining that there are many things, it denies that there is a whole composed of those things. We shall see, therefore, that philosophical propositions, instead of being concerned with the whole of things collectively, are concerned with all things distributively; and not only must they be concerned with all things, but they must be concerned with such properties of all things as do not depend upon the accidental nature of the things that there happen to be, but are true of any possible world, independently of such facts as can only be discovered by our senses.

This brings us to a second characteristic of philosophical propositions, namely, that they must be *a priori*. A philosophical proposition must be such as can be neither proved nor disproved by empirical evidence. Too often we find in philosophical books arguments based upon the course of history, or the convolutions of the brain, or the eyes of shell-fish. Special and accidental facts of this kind are irrelevant to philosophy, which must make only such assertions as would be equally true however the actual world were constituted.

We may sum up these two characteristics of philosophical propositions by saying that *philosophy is the science of the possible*. But this statement unexplained is liable to be misleading, since it may be thought that the possible is something other than the general, whereas in fact the two are indistinguishable.

Philosophy, if what has been said is correct, becomes indistinguishable from logic as that word has now come to be used. The study of logic consists, broadly speaking, of two not very sharply distinguished portions. On the one hand it is concerned with those general statements which can be made concerning everything without mentioning any one thing or predicate or relation, such for example as "if x is a member of the class α and every member of α is a member of β, then x is a member of the class β, whatever x, α, and β may be." On the other hand, it is concerned with the analysis and enumeration of logical *forms*, i.e. with the kinds of propositions that may occur, with the various types of facts, and with the classification of the constituents of facts. In this way logic provides an inventory of possibilities, a repertory of abstractly tenable hypotheses.

It might be thought that such a study would be too vague and too general to be of any very great importance, and that, if its problems became at any point sufficiently definite, they would be merged in the problems of some special science. It appears, however, that this is not the case. In some problems, for example, the analysis of space and time, the nature of perception, or the theory of judgment, the discovery of the logical form of the facts involved is the hardest part of the work and the part whose performance has been most lacking hitherto. It is chiefly for want of the right logical hypothesis that such problems have hitherto been treated in such an unsatisfactory manner, and have given rise to those contradictions or antinomies in which the enemies of reason among philosophers have at all times delighted.

By concentrating attention upon the investigation of logical forms, it becomes possible at last for philosophy to deal with its problems piecemeal, and to obtain, as the sciences do, such partial and probably not wholly correct results as subsequent investigation can utilise even while it supplements and improves them. Most philosophies hitherto have been constructed all in one block, in such a way that, if they were not wholly correct, they were wholly incorrect, and could not be used as a basis for further investigations. It is chiefly owing to this fact that philosophy, unlike science, has hitherto been unprogressive, because each original philosopher has had to begin the work again from the beginning, without being able to accept anything definite from the work of his predecessors. A scientific philosophy such as I wish to recommend will be piecemeal and tentative like other sciences; above all, it will be able to invent hypotheses which, even if they are not wholly true, will yet remain fruitful after the necessary corrections have been made. This possibility of successive approximations to the truth is, more than anything else, the source of the triumphs of science, and to transfer this possibility to philosophy is to ensure a progress in method whose importance it would be almost impossible to exaggerate.

The essence of philosophy as thus conceived is analysis, not synthesis. To build up systems of the world, like Heine's German professor who knit together fragments of life and made an intelligible system out of them, is not, I believe, any more feasible than the discovery of the philosopher's stone. What is feasible is the understanding of general forms, and the division of traditional problems into a number of separate and less baffling questions. "Divide and conquer" is the maxim of success here as elsewhere.

Let us illustrate these somewhat general maxims by examining their application to the philosophy of space, for it is only in application that the meaning or importance of a method can be understood. Suppose we are confronted with the problem of space as presented in Kant's Transcendental Æsthetic, and suppose we wish to discover what are the elements of the problem and what hope there is of obtaining a solution of them. It will soon appear that three entirely distinct problems, belonging to different studies, and requiring different methods for their solution, have been confusedly combined in the supposed single problem with which Kant is concerned. There is a problem of logic, a problem of physics, and a problem of theory of knowledge. Of these three, the problem of logic can be solved exactly and perfectly; the problem of physics can probably be solved with as great a degree of certainty and as great an approach to exactness as can be hoped in an empirical region; the problem of theory of knowledge, however, remains very obscure and very difficult to deal with. Let us see how these three problems arise.

(1) The logical problem has arisen through the suggestions of non-Euclidean geometry. Given a body of geometrical propositions, it is not difficult to find a minimum statement of the axioms from which this body of propositions can be deduced. It is also not difficult, by dropping or altering some of these axioms, to obtain a more general or a different geometry, having, from the point of view of pure mathematics, the same logical coherence and the same title to respect as the more familiar Euclidean geometry. The Euclidean geometry itself is true perhaps of actual space (though this is doubtful), but certainly of an infinite number of purely arithmetical systems, each of which, from the point of view of abstract logic, has an equal and indefeasible right to be called a Euclidean space. Thus space as an object of logical or mathematical study loses its uniqueness; not only are there many kinds of spaces, but there are an infinity of examples of each kind, though it is difficult to find any kind of which the space of physics may be an example, and it is impossible to find any kind of which the space of physics is certainly an example. As an illustration of one possible logical system of geometry we may consider all relations of three terms which are analogous in certain formal respects to the relation

"between" as it appears to be in actual space. A space is then defined by means of one such three-term relation. The points of the space are all the terms which have this relation to something or other, and their order in the space in question is determined by this relation. The points of one space are necessarily also points of other spaces, since there are necessarily other three-term relations having those same points for their field. The space in fact is not determined by the class of its points, but by the ordering three-term relation. When enough abstract logical properties of such relations have been enumerated to determine the resulting kind of geometry, say, for example, Euclidean geometry, it becomes unnecessary for the pure geometer in his abstract capacity to distinguish between the various relations which have all these properties. He considers the whole class of such relations, not any single one among them. Thus in studying a given kind of geometry the pure mathematician is studying a certain class of relations defined by means of certain abstract logical properties which take the place of what used to be called axioms. The nature of geometrical *reasoning* therefore is purely deductive and purely logical; if any special epistemological peculiarities are to be found in geometry, it must not be in the reasoning, but in our knowledge concerning the axioms in some given space.

(2) The physical problem of space is both more interesting and more difficult than the logical problem. The physical problem may be stated as follows: to find in the physical world, or to construct from physical materials, a space of one of the kinds enumerated by the logical treatment of geometry. This problem derives its difficulty from the attempt to accommodate to the roughness and vagueness of the real world some system possessing the logical clearness and exactitude of pure mathematics. That this can be done with a certain degree of approximation is fairly evident If I see three people A, B, and C sitting in a row, I become aware of the fact which may be expressed by saying that B is between A and C rather than that A is between B and C, or C is between A and B. This relation of "between" which is thus perceived to hold has some of the abstract logical properties of those three-term relations which, we saw, give rise to a geometry, but its properties fail to be exact, and are not, as empirically given, amenable to the kind of

treatment at which geometry aims. In abstract geometry we deal with points, straight lines, and planes; but the three people A, B, and C whom I see sitting in a row are not exactly points, nor is the row exactly a straight line. Nevertheless physics, which formally assumes a space containing points, straight lines, and planes, is found empirically to give results applicable to the sensible world. It must therefore be possible to find an interpretation of the points, straight lines, and planes of physics in terms of physical data, or at any rate in terms of data together with such hypothetical additions as seem least open to question. Since all data suffer from a lack of mathematical precision through being of a certain size and somewhat vague in outline, it is plain that if such a notion as that of a point is to find any application to empirical material, the point must be neither a datum nor a hypothetical addition to data, but a *construction* by means of data with their hypothetical additions. It is obvious that any hypothetical filling out of data is less dubious and unsatisfactory when the additions are closely analogous to data than when they are of a radically different sort. To assume, for example, that objects which we see continue, after we have turned away our eyes, to be more or less analogous to what they were while we were looking, is a less violent assumption than to assume that such objects are composed of an infinite number of mathematical points. Hence in the physical study of the geometry of physical space, points must not be assumed *ab initio* as they are in the logical treatment of geometry, but must be constructed as systems composed of data and hypothetical analogues of data. We are thus led naturally to define a physical point as a certain class of those objects which are the ultimate constituents of the physical world. It will be the class of all those objects which, as one would naturally say, *contain* the point. To secure a definition giving this result, without previously assuming that physical objects are composed of points, is an agreeable problem in mathematical logic. The solution of this problem and the perception of its importance are due to my friend Dr. Whitehead. The oddity of regarding a point as a class of physical entities wears off with familiarity, and ought in any case not to be felt by those who maintain, as practically every one does, that points are mathematical fictions. The word "fiction" is used glibly in such connexions by many men who seem not to feel the necessity of explaining how it can come about that a fiction can be so useful in the study of the actual world as the points of mathematical physics have been found to be. By our definition, which regards a point as a class of physical objects, it is explained both how the use of points can lead to important physical results, and how we can nevertheless avoid the assumption that points are themselves entities in the physical world.

Many of the mathematically convenient properties of abstract logical spaces cannot be either known to belong or known not to belong to the space of physics. Such are all the properties connected with continuity. For to know that actual space has these properties would require an infinite exactness of sense-perception. If actual space is continuous, there are nevertheless many possible non-continuous spaces which will be empirically indistinguishable from it; and, conversely, actual space may be non-continuous and yet empirically indistinguishable from a possible continuous space. Continuity, therefore, though obtainable in the *a priori* region of arithmetic, is not with certainty obtainable in the space or time of the physical world: whether these are continuous or not would seem to be a question not only unanswered but for ever unanswerable. From the point of view of philosophy, however, the discovery that a question is unanswerable is as complete an answer as any that could possibly be obtained. And from the point of view of physics, where no empirical means of distinction can be found, there can be no empirical objection to the mathematically simplest assumption, which is that of continuity.

The subject of the physical theory of space is a very large one, hitherto little explored. It is associated with a similar theory of time, and both have been forced upon the attention of philosophically minded physicists by the discussions which have raged concerning the theory of relativity.

(3) The problem with which Kant is concerned in the Transcendental Æsthetic is primarily the epistemological problem: "How do we come to have knowledge of geometry *a priori*?" By the distinction between the logical and physical problems of geometry, the bearing and scope of this question are greatly altered. Our knowledge of pure geometry is *a priori* but is

wholly logical. Our knowledge of physical geometry is synthetic, but is not *a priori*. Our knowledge of pure geometry is hypothetical, and does not enable us to assert, for example, that the axiom of parallels is true in the physical world. Our knowledge of physical geometry, while it does enable us to assert that this axiom is approximately verified, does not, owing to the inevitable inexactitude of observation, enable us to assert that it is verified *exactly*. Thus, with the separation which we have made between pure geometry and the geometry of physics, the Kantian problem collapses. To the question, "How is synthetic *a priori* knowledge possible?" we can now reply, at any rate so far as geometry is concerned, "It is not possible," if "synthetic" means "not deducible from logic alone." Our knowledge of geometry, like the rest of our knowledge, is derived partly from logic, partly from sense, and the peculiar position which in Kant's day geometry appeared to occupy is seen now to be a delusion. There are still some philosophers, it is true, who maintain that our knowledge that the axiom of parallels, for example, is true of actual space, is not to be accounted for empirically, but is as Kant maintained derived from an *a priori* intuition. This position is not logically refutable, but I think it loses all plausibility as soon as we realise how complicated and derivative is the notion of physical space. As we have seen, the application of geometry to the physical world in no way demands that there should really be points and straight lines among physical entities. The principle of economy, therefore, demands that we should abstain from assuming the existence of points and straight lines. As soon, however, as we accept the view that points and straight lines are complicated constructions by means of classes of physical entities, the hypothesis that we have an *a priori* intuition enabling us to know what happens to straight lines when they are produced indefinitely becomes extremely strained and harsh; nor do I think that such an hypothesis would ever have arisen in the mind of a philosopher who had grasped the nature of physical space. Kant, under the influence of Newton, adopted, though with some vacillation, the hypothesis of absolute space, and this hypothesis, though logically unobjectionable, is removed by Occam's razor, since absolute space is an unnecessary entity in the explanation of the physical world. Although, therefore, we cannot refute the Kantian theory of an *a priori* intuition, we can remove its grounds one by one through an analysis of the problem. Thus, here as in many other philosophical questions, the analytic method, while not capable of arriving at a demonstrative result, is nevertheless capable of showing that all the positive grounds in favour of a certain theory are fallacious and that a less unnatural theory is capable of accounting for the facts.

Another question by which the capacity of the analytic method can be shown is the question of realism. Both those who advocate and those who combat realism seem to me to be far from clear as to the nature of the problem which they are discussing. If we ask: "Are our objects of perception *real* and are they *independent* of the percipient?" it must be supposed that we attach some meaning to the words "real" and "independent," and yet, if either side in the controversy of realism is asked to define these two words, their answer is pretty sure to embody confusions such as logical analysis will reveal.

Let us begin with the word "real." There certainly are objects of perception, and therefore, if the question whether these objects are real is to be a substantial question, there must be in the world two sorts of objects, namely, the real and the unreal, and yet the unreal is supposed to be essentially what there is not. The question what properties must belong to an object in order to make it real is one to which an adequate answer is seldom if ever forthcoming. There is of course the Hegelian answer, that the real is the self-consistent and that nothing is self-consistent except the Whole; but this answer, true or false, is not relevant in our present discussion, which moves on a lower plane and is concerned with the status of objects of perception among other objects of equal fragmentariness. Objects of perception are contrasted, in the discussions concerning realism, rather with psychical states on the one hand and matter on the other hand than with the all-inclusive whole of things. The question we have therefore to consider is the question as to what can be meant by assigning "reality" to some but not all of the entities that make up the world. Two elements, I think, make up what is felt rather than thought when the word "reality" is used in this sense. A thing is real if it persists at times when it is not perceived; or again, a thing is real when it is correlated with other things in a way which experience has led us to expect. It will be seen that reality in either of these senses is by no means necessary to a thing, and that in fact there might be a whole world in which nothing was real in either of these senses. It might turn out that the objects of perception failed of reality in one or both of these respects, without its being in any way deducible that they are not parts of the external world with which physics deals. Similar remarks will apply to the word "independent." Most of the associations of this word are bound up with ideas as to causation which it is not now possible to maintain. A is independent of B when B is not an indispensable part of the *cause* of A. But when it is recognised that causation is nothing more than correlation, and that there are correlations of simultaneity as well as of succession, it becomes evident that there is no uniqueness in a series of casual antecedents of a given event, but that, at any point where there is a correlation of simultaneity, we can pass from one line of antecedents to another in order to obtain a new series of causal antecedents. It will be necessary to specify the causal law according to which the antecedents are to be considered. I received a letter the other day from a correspondent who had been puzzled by various philosophical questions. After enumerating them he says: "These questions led me from Bonn to Strassburg, where I found Professor Simmel." Now, it would be absurd to deny that these questions caused his body to move from Bonn to Strassburg, and yet it must be supposed that a set of purely mechanical antecedents could also be found which would account for this transfer of matter from one place to another. Owing to this plurality of causal series antecedent to a given event, the notion of *the* cause becomes indefinite, and the question of independence becomes correspondingly ambiguous. Thus, instead of asking simply whether A is independent of B, we ought to ask whether there is a series determined by such and such causal laws leading from B to A. This point is important in connexion with the particular question of objects of perception. It may be that no objects quite like those which we perceive ever exist unperceived; in this case there will be a causal law according to which objects of perception are not independent of being perceived. But even if this be the case, it may nevertheless also happen that there are purely physical causal laws determining the occurrence of objects which are perceived by means of other objects which perhaps are not perceived. In that case, in regard to such causal laws objects of perception will be independent of being perceived. Thus the question whether objects of perception are independent of being perceived is, as it stands, indeterminate, and the answer will be yes or no according to the method adopted of making it determinate. I believe that this confusion has borne a very large part in prolonging the controversies on this subject, which might well have seemed capable of remaining for ever undecided. The view which I should wish to advocate is that objects of perception do not persist unchanged at times when they are not perceived, although probably objects more or less resembling them do exist at such times; that objects of perception are part, and the only empirically knowable part, of the actual subject-matter of physics, and are themselves properly to be called physical; that purely physical laws exist determining the character and duration of objects of perception without any reference to the fact that they are perceived; and that in the establishment of such laws the propositions of physics do not presuppose any propositions of psychology or even the existence of mind. I do not know whether realists would recognise such a view as realism. All that I should claim for it is, that it avoids difficulties which seem to me to beset both realism and idealism as hitherto advocated, and that it avoids the appeal which they have made to ideas which logical analysis shows to be ambiguous. A further defence and elaboration of the positions which I advocate, but for which time is lacking now, will be found indicated in my book on *Our Knowledge of the External World*.[22]

The adoption of scientific method in philosophy, if I am not mistaken, compels us to abandon the hope of solving many of the more ambitious and humanly interesting problems of traditional philosophy. Some of these it relegates, though with little expectation of a successful solution, to special sciences, others it shows to be such as our capacities are essentially incapable of solving. But there remain a large number of the recognised problems of philosophy in regard to which the method advocated gives all those advantages of division into distinct questions, of tentative, partial, and progressive advance, and of appeal to principles with which, independently of temperament, all competent students must agree. The failure of philosophy hitherto has been due in the main to haste and ambition: patience and modesty, here as in other sciences, will open the road to solid and durable progress.

Footnotes

[19] Bosanquet, *Logic*, ii, p. 211.

[20] *Some Problems of Philosophy*, p 124.

[21] *First Principles* (1862), Part II, beginning of chap. viii.

[22] Open Court Company, 1914.

<

div class="footnote">

7 8

7.

8.

Chapter 7

The Ultimate Constituents of Matter

[23]

I wish to discuss in this article no less a question than the ancient metaphysical query, "What is matter?" The question, "What is matter?" in so far as it concerns philosophy, is, I think, already capable of an answer which in principle will be as complete as an answer can hope to be; that is to say, we can separate the problem into an essentially soluble and an essentially insoluble portion, and we can now see how to solve the essentially soluble portion, at least as regards its main outlines. It is these outlines which I wish to suggest in the present article. My main position, which is realistic, is, I hope and believe, not remote from that of Professor Alexander, by whose writings on this subject I have profited greatly.[24] It is also in close accord with that of Dr. Nunn.[25]

Common sense is accustomed to the division of the world into mind and matter. It is supposed by all who have never studied philosophy that the distinction between mind and matter is perfectly clear and easy, that the two do not at any point overlap, and that only a fool or a philosopher could be in doubt as to whether any given entity is mental or material. This simple faith survives in Descartes and in a somewhat modified form in Spinoza, but with Leibniz it begins to disappear, and from his day to our own almost every philosopher of note has criticised and rejected the dualism of common sense. It is my intention in this article to defend this dualism; but before defending it we must spend a few moments on the reasons which have prompted its rejection.

Our knowledge of the material world is obtained by means of the senses, of sight and touch and so on. At first it is supposed that things are just as they seem, but two opposite sophistications soon destroy this naïve belief. On the one hand the physicists cut up matter into molecules, atoms, corpuscles, and as many more such subdivisions as their future needs may make them postulate, and the units at which they arrive are uncommonly different from the visible, tangible objects of daily life. A unit of matter tends more and more to be something like an electromagnetic field filling all space, though having its greatest intensity in a small region. Matter consisting of such elements is as remote from daily life as any metaphysical theory. It differs from the theories of metaphysicians only in the fact that its practical efficacy proves that it contains some measure of truth and induces business men to invest money on the strength of it; but, in spite of its connection with the money market, it remains a metaphysical theory none the less.

The second kind of sophistication to which the world of common sense has been subjected is derived from the psychologists and physiologists. The physiologists point out that what we see depends upon the eye, that what we hear depends upon the ear, and that all our senses are liable to be affected by anything which affects the brain, like alcohol or hasheesh. Psychologists point out how much of what we think we see is supplied by association or unconscious inference, how much is mental interpretation, and how doubtful is the residuum which can be regarded as crude datum. From these facts it is argued by the psychologists that the notion of a datum passively received by the mind is a delusion, and it is argued by the physiologists that even if a pure datum of sense could be obtained by the analysis of experience, still this datum could not belong, as common sense supposes, to the outer world, since its whole nature is conditioned by our nerves and sense organs, changing as they change in ways which it is thought impossible to connect with any change in the matter supposed to be perceived. This physiologist's argument is exposed to the rejoinder, more specious than solid, that our knowledge of the existence of the sense organs and nerves is obtained by that very process which the physiologist has been engaged in discrediting, since the existence of the nerves and sense organs is only known through the evidence of the senses themselves. This argument may prove that some reinterpretation of the results of physiology is necessary before they can acquire metaphysical validity. But it does not upset the physiological argument in so far as this constitutes merely a *reductio ad absurdum* of naïve realism.

These various lines of argument prove, I think, that some part of the beliefs of common sense must be abandoned. They prove that, if we take these beliefs as a whole, we are forced into conclusions which are in part self-contradictory; but such arguments cannot of themselves decide what portion of our common-sense beliefs is in need of correction. Common sense believes that what we see is physical, outside the mind, and continuing to exist if we shut our eyes or turn them in another direction. I believe that common sense is right in regarding what we see as physical and (in one of several possible senses) outside the mind, but is probably wrong in supposing that it continues to exist when we are no longer looking at it. It seems to me that the whole discussion of matter has been obscured by two errors which support each other. The first of these is the error that what we see, or perceive through any of our other senses, is subjective: the second is the belief that what is physical must be persistent. Whatever physics may regard as the ultimate constituents of matter, it always supposes these constituents to be indestructible. Since the immediate data of sense are not indestructible but in a state of perpetual flux, it is argued that these data themselves cannot be among the ultimate constituents of matter. I believe this to be a sheer mistake. The persistent particles of mathematical physics I regard as logical constructions, symbolic fictions enabling us to express compendiously very complicated assemblages of facts; and, on the other hand, I believe that the actual data in sensation, the immediate objects of sight or touch or hearing, are extra-mental, purely physical, and among the ultimate constituents of matter.

My meaning in regard to the impermanence of physical entities may perhaps be made clearer by the use of Bergson's favourite illustration of the cinematograph. When I first read Bergson's statement that the mathematician conceives the world after the analogy of a cinematograph, I had never seen a cinematograph, and my first visit to one was determined by the desire to verify Bergson's statement, which I found to be completely true, at least so far as I am concerned. When, in a picture palace, we see a man rolling down hill, or running away from the police, or falling into a river, or doing any of those other things to which men in such places are addicted, we know that there is not really only one man moving, but a succession of films, each with a different momentary man. The illusion of persistence arises only through the approach to continuity in the series of momentary men. Now what I wish to suggest is that in this respect the cinema is a better metaphysician than common sense, physics, or philosophy. The real man too, I believe, however the police may swear to his identity, is really a series of momentary men, each different one from the other, and bound together, not by a numerical identity, but by continuity and certain intrinsic causal laws. And what applies to men applies equally to tables and chairs, the sun, moon and stars. Each of these is to be regarded, not as one single persistent entity, but as a series of entities succeeding each other in time, each lasting for a very brief period, though probably not for a mere mathematical instant. In saying this I am only urging the same kind of division in time as we are accustomed to acknowledge in the case of space. A body which fills a cubic foot will be admitted to consist of many smaller bodies, each occupying only a very tiny volume; similarly a thing which persists for an hour is to be regarded as composed of many things of less duration. A true theory of matter requires a division of things into time-corpuscles as well as into space-corpuscles.

The world may be conceived as consisting of a multitude of entities arranged in a certain pattern. The entities which are arranged I shall call "particulars." The arrangement or pattern results from relations among particulars. Classes or series of particulars, collected together on account of some property which makes it convenient to be able to speak of them as wholes, are what I call logical constructions or symbolic fictions. The particulars are to be conceived, not on the analogy of bricks in a building, but rather on the analogy of notes in a symphony. The ultimate constituents of a symphony (apart from relations) are the notes, each of which lasts only for a very short time. We may collect together all the notes played by one instrument: these may be regarded as the analogues of the successive particulars which common sense would regard as successive states of one "thing." But the "thing" ought to be regarded as no more "real" or "substantial" than, for example, the rôle of the trombone. As soon as "things" are conceived in this manner it will be found that the difficulties in the way of regarding immediate objects of sense as physical have largely disappeared.

When people ask, "Is the object of sense mental or physical?" they seldom have any clear idea either what is meant by "mental" or "physical," or what criteria are to be applied for deciding whether a given entity belongs to one class or the other. I do not know how to give a sharp definition of the word "mental," but something may be done by enumerating occurrences which are indubitably mental: believing, doubting, wishing, willing, being pleased or pained, are certainly mental occurrences; so are what we may call experiences, seeing, hearing, smelling, perceiving generally. But it does not follow from this that what is seen, what is heard, what is smelt, what is perceived, must be mental. When I see a flash of lightning, my seeing of it is mental, but what I see, although it is not quite the same as what anybody else sees at the same moment, and although it seems very unlike what the physicist would describe as a flash of lightning, is not mental. I maintain, in fact, that if the physicist could describe truly and fully all that occurs in the physical world when there is a flash of lightning, it would contain as a constituent what I see, and also what is seen by anybody else who would commonly be said to see the same flash. What I mean may perhaps be made plainer by saying that if my body could remain in exactly the same state in which it is, although my mind had ceased to exist, precisely that object which I now see when I see the flash would exist, although of course I should not see it, since my seeing is mental. The principal reasons which have led people to reject this view have, I think, been two: first, that they did not adequately distinguish between my seeing and what I see; secondly, that the causal dependence of what I see upon my body has made people suppose that what I see cannot be "outside" me. The first of these reasons need not detain us, since the confusion only needs to be pointed out in order to be obviated; but the second requires some discussion, since it can only be answered by removing current misconceptions, on the one hand as to the nature of space, and on the other, as to the meaning of causal dependence.

When people ask whether colours, for example, or other secondary qualities are inside or outside the mind, they seem to suppose that their meaning must be clear, and that it ought to be possible to say yes or no without any further discussion of the terms involved. In fact, however, such terms as "inside" or "outside" are very ambiguous. What is meant by asking whether this or that is "in" the mind? The mind is not like a bag or a pie; it does not occupy a certain region in space, or, if (in a sense) it does, what is in that region is presumably part of the brain, which would not be said to be in the mind. When people say that sensible qualities are in the mind, they do not mean "spatially contained in" in the sense in which the blackbirds were in the pie. We might regard the mind as an assemblage of particulars, namely, what would be called "states of mind," which would belong together in virtue of some specific common quality. The common quality of all states of mind would be the quality designated by the word "mental"; and besides this we should have to suppose that each separate person's states of mind have some common characteristic distinguishing them from the states of mind of other people. Ignoring this latter point, let us ask ourselves whether the quality designated by the word "mental" does, as a matter of observation, actually belong to objects of sense, such as colours or noises. I think any candid person must reply that, however difficult it may be to know what we mean by "mental," it is not difficult to see that colours and noises are not mental in the sense of having that intrinsic peculiarity which belongs to beliefs and wishes and volitions, but not to the physical world. Berkeley advances on this subject a plausible argument[26] which seems to me to rest upon an ambiguity in the word "pain." He argues that the realist supposes the heat which he feels in approaching a fire to be something outside his mind, but that as he approaches nearer and nearer to the fire the sensation of heat passes imperceptibly into pain, and that no one could regard pain as something outside the mind. In reply to this argument, it should be observed in the first place that the heat of which we are immediately aware is not in the fire but in our own body. It is only by inference that the fire is judged to be the cause of the heat which we feel in our body. In the second place (and this is the more important point), when we speak of pain we may mean one of two things: we may mean the object of the sensation or other experience which has the quality of being painful, or we may mean the quality of painfulness itself. When a man says he has a pain in his great toe, what he means is that he has a sensation associated with his great toe and having the quality of painfulness. The sensation itself, like every sensation, consists in experiencing a sensible object, and the experiencing has that quality of painfulness which only mental occurrences can have, but which may belong to thoughts or desires, as well as to sensations. But in common language we speak of the sensible object experienced in a painful sensation as a pain, and it is this way of speaking which causes the confusion upon which the plausibility of Berkeley's argument depends. It would be absurd to attribute the quality of painfulness to anything non-mental, and hence it comes to be thought that what we call a pain in the toe must be mental. In fact, however, it is not the sensible object in such a case which is painful, but the sensation, that is to say, the experience of the sensible object. As the heat which we experience from the fire grows greater, the experience passes gradually from being pleasant to being painful, but neither the pleasure nor the pain is a quality of the object experienced as opposed to the experience, and it is therefore a fallacy to argue that this object must be mental on the ground that painfulness can only be attributed to what is mental.

If, then, when we say that something is in the mind we mean that it has a certain recognisable intrinsic characteristic such as belongs to thoughts and desires, it must be maintained on grounds of immediate inspection that objects of sense are not in any mind.

A different meaning of "in the mind" is, however, to be inferred from the arguments advanced by those who regard sensible objects as being in the mind. The arguments used are, in the main, such as would prove the causal dependence of objects of sense upon the percipient. Now the notion of causal dependence is very obscure and difficult, much more so in fact than is generally realised by philosophers. I shall return to this point in a moment. For the present, however, accepting the notion of causal dependence without criticism, I wish to urge that the dependence in question is rather upon our bodies than upon our minds. The visual appearance of an object is altered if we shut one eye, or squint, or look previously at something dazzling; but all these are bodily acts, and the alterations which they effect are to be explained by physiology and optics, not by psychology.[27] They are in fact of exactly the same kind as the alterations effected by spectacles or a microscope. They belong therefore to the theory of the physical world, and can have no bearing upon the question whether what we see is causally dependent upon the mind. What they do tend to prove, and what I for my part have no wish to deny, is that what we see is causally dependent upon our body and is not, as crude common sense would suppose, something which would exist equally if our eyes and nerves and brain were absent, any more than the visual appearance presented by an object seen through a microscope would remain if the microscope were removed. So long as it is supposed that the physical world is composed of stable and more or less permanent constituents, the fact that what we see is changed by changes in our body appears to afford reason for regarding what we see as not an ultimate constituent of matter. But if it is recognised that the ultimate constituents of matter are as circumscribed in duration as in spatial extent, the whole of this difficulty vanishes.

There remains, however, another difficulty, connected with space. When we look at the sun we wish to know something about the sun itself, which is ninety-three million miles away; but what we see is dependent upon our eyes, and it is difficult to suppose that our eyes can affect what happens at a distance of ninety-three million miles. Physics tells us that certain electromagnetic waves start from the sun, and reach our eyes after about eight minutes. They there produce disturbances in the rods and cones, thence in the optic nerve, thence in the brain. At the end of this purely physical series, by some odd miracle, comes the experience which we call "seeing the sun," and it is such experiences which form the whole and sole reason for our belief in the optic nerve, the rods and cones, the ninety-three million miles, the electromagnetic waves, and the sun itself. It is this curious oppositeness of direction between the order of causation as affirmed by physics, and the order of evidence as revealed by theory of knowledge, that causes the most serious perplexities in regard to the nature of physical reality. Anything that invalidates our seeing, as a source of knowledge concerning physical reality, invalidates also the whole of physics and physiology. And yet, starting from a common-sense acceptance of our seeing, physics has been led step by step to the construction of the causal chain in which our seeing is the last link, and the immediate object which we see cannot be regarded as that initial cause which we believe to be ninety-three million miles away, and which we are inclined to regard as the "real" sun.

I have stated this difficulty as forcibly as I can, because I believe that it can only be answered by a radical analysis and reconstruction of all the conceptions upon whose employment it depends.

Space, time, matter and cause, are the chief of these conceptions. Let us begin with the conception of cause.

Causal dependence, as I observed a moment ago, is a conception which it is very dangerous to accept at its face value. There exists a notion that in regard to any event there is something which may be called *the* cause of that event—some one definite occurrence, without which the event would have been impossible and with which it becomes necessary. An event is supposed to be dependent upon its cause in some way which in it is not dependent upon other things. Thus men will urge that the mind is dependent upon the brain, or, with equal plausibility, that the brain is dependent upon the mind. It seems not improbable that if we had sufficient knowledge we could infer the state of a man's mind from the state of his brain, or the state of his brain from the state of his mind. So long as the usual conception of causal dependence is retained, this state of affairs can be used by the materialist to urge that the state of our brain causes our thoughts, and by the idealist to urge that our thoughts cause the state of our brain. Either contention is equally valid or equally invalid. The fact seems to be that there are many correlations of the sort which may be called causal, and that, for example, either a physical or a mental event can be predicted, theoretically, either from a sufficient number of physical antecedents or from a sufficient number of mental antecedents. To speak of *the* cause of an event is therefore misleading. Any set of antecedents from which the event can theoretically be inferred by means of correlations might be called a cause of the event. But to speak of *the* cause is to imply a uniqueness which does not exist.

The relevance of this to the experience which we call "seeing the sun" is obvious. The fact that there exists a chain of antecedents which makes our seeing dependent upon the eyes and nerves and brain does not even tend to show that there is not another chain of antecedents in which the eyes and nerves and brain as physical things are ignored. If we are to escape from the dilemma which seemed to arise out of the physiological causation of what we see when we say we see the sun, we must find, at least in theory, a way of stating causal laws for the physical world, in which the units are not material things, such as the eyes and nerves and brain, but momentary particulars of the same sort as our momentary visual object when we look at the sun. The sun itself and the eyes and nerves and brain must be regarded as assemblages of momentary particulars. Instead of supposing, as we naturally do when we start from an uncritical acceptance of the apparent dicta of physics, that *matter* is what is "really real" in the physical world, and that the immediate objects of sense are mere phantasms, we must regard matter as a logical construction, of which the constituents will be just such evanescent particulars as may, when an observer happens to be present, become data of sense to that observer. What physics regards as the sun of eight minutes ago will be a whole assemblage of particulars, existing at different times, spreading out from a centre with the velocity of light, and containing among their number all those visual data which are seen by people who are now looking at the sun. Thus the sun of eight minutes ago is a class of particulars, and what I see when I now look at the sun is one member of this class. The various particulars constituting this class will be correlated with each other by a certain continuity and certain intrinsic laws of variation as we pass outwards from the centre, together with certain modifications correlated extrinsically with other particulars which are not members of this class. It is these extrinsic modifications which represent the sort of facts that, in our former account, appeared as the influence of the eyes and nerves in modifying the appearance of the sun.[28]

The *prima facie* difficulties in the way of this view are chiefly derived from an unduly conventional theory of space. It might seem at first sight as if we had packed the world much fuller than it could possibly hold. At every place between us and the sun, we said, there is to be a particular which is to be a member of the sun as it was a few minutes ago. There will also, of course, have to be a particular which is a member of any planet or fixed star that may happen to be visible from that place. At the place where I am, there will be particulars which will be members severally of all the "things" I am now said to be perceiving. Thus throughout the world, everywhere, there will be an enormous number of particulars coexisting in the same place. But these troubles result from contenting ourselves too readily with the merely three-dimensional space to which schoolmasters have accustomed us. The space of the real world is a space of six dimensions, and as soon as we realise this we see that there is plenty of room for all the particulars for which we want to find positions. In order to realise this we have only to return for a moment from the polished space of physics to the rough and untidy space of our immediate sensible experience. The space of one man's sensible objects is a three-dimensional space. It does not appear probable that two men ever both perceive at the same time any one sensible object; when they are said to see the same thing or hear the same noise, there will always be some difference, however slight, between the actual shapes seen or the actual sounds heard. If this is so, and if, as is generally assumed, position in space is purely relative, it follows that the space of one man's objects and the space of another man's objects have no place in common, that they are in fact different spaces, and not merely different parts of one space. I mean by this that such immediate spatial relations as are perceived to hold between the different parts of the sensible space perceived by one man, do not hold between parts of sensible spaces perceived by different men. There are therefore a multitude of three-dimensional spaces in the world: there are all those perceived by observers, and presumably also those which are not perceived, merely because no observer is suitably situated for perceiving them.

But although these spaces do not have to one another the same kind of spatial relations as obtain between the parts of one of them, it is nevertheless possible to arrange these spaces themselves in a three-dimensional order. This is done by means of the correlated particulars which we regard as members (or aspects) of one physical thing. When a number of people are said to see the same object, those who would be said to be near to the object see a particular occupying a larger part of their field of vision than is occupied by the corresponding particular seen by people who would be said to be farther from the thing. By means of such considerations it is possible, in ways which need not now be further specified, to arrange all the different spaces in a three-dimensional series. Since each of the spaces is itself three-dimensional, the whole world of particulars is thus arranged in a six-dimensional space, that is to say, six co-ordinates will be required to assign completely the position of any given particular, namely, three to assign its position in its own space and three more to assign the position of its space among the other spaces.

There are two ways of classifying particulars: we may take together all those that belong to a given "perspective," or all those that are, as common sense would say, different "aspects" of the same "thing." For example, if I am (as is said) seeing the sun, what I see belongs to two assemblages: (1) the as-semblage of all my present objects of sense, which is what I call a "perspective"; (2) the assemblage of all the different par-ticulars which would be called aspects of the sun of eight minutes ago—this assemblage is what I define as *being* the sun of eight minutes ago. Thus "perspectives" and "things" are merely two different ways of classifying particulars. It is to be observed that there is no *a priori* necessity for particulars to be susceptible of this double classification. There may be what might be called "wild" particulars, not having the usual rela-tions by which the classification is effected; perhaps dreams and hallucinations are composed of particulars which are "wild" in this sense.

The exact definition of what is meant by a perspective is not quite easy. So long as we confine ourselves to visible objects or to objects of touch we might define the perspective of a given particular as "all particulars which have a simple (direct) spa-tial relation to the given particular." Between two patches of colour which I see now, there is a direct spatial relation which

I equally see. But between patches of colour seen by different men there is only an indirect constructed spatial relation by means of the placing of "things" in physical space (which is the same as the space composed of perspectives). Those particulars which have direct spatial relations to a given particular will belong to the same perspective. But if, for example, the sounds which I hear are to belong to the same perspective with the patches of colour which I see, there must be particulars which have no direct spatial relation and yet belong to the same perspective. We cannot define a perspective as all the data of one percipient at one time, because we wish to allow the possibility of perspectives which are not perceived by any one. There will be need, therefore, in defining a perspective, of some principle derived neither from psychology nor from space.

Such a principle may be obtained from the consideration of *time*. The one all-embracing time, like the one all-embracing space, is a construction; there is no *direct* time-relation between particulars belonging to my perspective and particulars belonging to another man's. On the other hand, any two particulars of which I am aware are either simultaneous or successive, and their simultaneity or successiveness is sometimes itself a datum to me. We may therefore define the perspective to which a given particular belongs as "all particulars simultaneous with the given particular," where "simultaneous" is to be understood as a direct simple relation, not the derivative constructed relation of physics. It may be observed that the introduction of "local time" suggested by the principle of relativity has effected, for purely scientific reasons, much the same multiplication of times as we have just been advocating.

The sum-total of all the particulars that are (directly) either simultaneous with or before or after a given particular may be defined as the "biography" to which that particular belongs. It will be observed that, just as a perspective need not be actually perceived by any one, so a biography need not be actually lived by any one. Those biographies that are lived by no one are called "official."

The definition of a "thing" is effected by means of continuity and of correlations which have a certain differential independence of other "things." That is to say, given a particular in one perspective, there will usually in a neighbouring perspective be a very similar particular, differing from the given particular, to the first order of small quantities, according to a law involving only the difference of position of the two perspectives in perspective space, and not any of the other "things" in the universe. It is this continuity and differential independence in the law of change as we pass from one perspective to another that defines the class of particulars which is to be called "one thing."

Broadly speaking, we may say that the physicist finds it convenient to classify particulars into "things," while the psychologist finds it convenient to classify them into "perspectives" and "biographies," since one perspective *may* constitute the momentary data of one percipient, and one biography *may* constitute the whole of the data of one percipient throughout his life.

We may now sum up our discussion. Our object has been to discover as far as possible the nature of the ultimate constituents of the physical world. When I speak of the "physical world," I mean, to begin with, the world dealt with by physics. It is obvious that physics is an empirical science, giving us a certain amount of knowledge and based upon evidence obtained through the senses. But partly through the development of physics itself, partly through arguments derived from physiology, psychology or metaphysics, it has come to be thought that the immediate data of sense could not themselves form part of the ultimate constituents of the physical world, but were in some sense "mental," "in the mind," or "subjective." The grounds for this view, in so far as they depend upon physics, can only be adequately dealt with by rather elaborate constructions depending upon symbolic logic, showing that out of such materials as are provided by the senses it is possible to construct classes and series having the properties which physics assigns to matter. Since this argument is difficult and technical, I have not embarked upon it in this article. But in so far as the view that sense-data are "mental" rests upon physiology, psychology, or metaphysics, I have tried to show that it rests upon confusions and prejudices—prejudices in favour of permanence in the ultimate constituents of matter, and confusions derived from unduly simple notions as to space, from the causal correlation of sense-data with sense-organs, and from failure to distinguish between sense-data and sensations. If what we have said on these subjects is valid, the existence of sense-data is logically independent of the existence of mind, and is causally dependent upon the *body* of the percipient rather than upon his mind. The causal dependence upon the body of the percipient, we found, is a more complicated matter than it appears to be, and, like all causal dependence, is apt to give rise to erroneous beliefs through misconceptions as to the nature of causal correlation. If we have been right in our contentions, sense-data are merely those among the ultimate constituents of the physical world, of which we happen to be immediately aware; they themselves are purely physical, and all that is mental in connection with them is our awareness of them, which is irrelevant to their nature and to their place in physics.

Unduly simple notions as to space have been a great stumbling-block to realists. When two men look at the same table, it is supposed that what the one sees and what the other sees are in the same place. Since the shape and colour are not quite the same for the two men, this raises a difficulty, hastily solved, or rather covered up, by declaring what each sees to be purely "subjective"—though it would puzzle those who use this glib word to say what they mean by it. The truth seems to be that space—and time also—is much more complicated than it would appear to be from the finished structure of physics, and that the one all-embracing three-dimensional space is a logical construction, obtained by means of correlations from a crude space of six dimensions. The particulars occupying this six-dimensional space, classified in one way, form "things," from which with certain further manipulations we can obtain what physics can regard as matter; classified in another way, they form "perspectives" and "biographies," which may, if a suitable percipient happens to exist, form respectively the sense-data of a momentary or of a total experience. It is only when physical "things" have been dissected into series of classes of particulars, as we have done, that the conflict between the point of view of physics and the point of view of psychology can be overcome. This conflict, if what has been said is not mistaken, flows from different methods of classification, and vanishes as soon as its source is discovered.

In favour of the theory which I have briefly outlined, I do not claim that it is *certainly* true. Apart from the likelihood of mistakes, much of it is avowedly hypothetical. What I do claim for the theory is that it *may* be true, and that this is more than can be said for any other theory except the closely analogous theory of Leibniz. The difficulties besetting realism, the confusions obstructing any philosophical account of physics, the dilemma resulting from discrediting sense-data, which yet remain the sole source of our knowledge of the outer world—all these are avoided by the theory which I advocate. This does not prove the theory to be true, since probably many other theories might be invented which would have the same merits. But it does prove that the theory has a better chance of being true than any of its present competitors, and it suggests that what can be known with certainty is likely to be discoverable by taking our theory as a starting-point, and gradually freeing it from all such assumptions as seem irrelevant, unnecessary, or unfounded. On these grounds, I recommend it to attention as a hypothesis and a basis for further work, though not as itself a finished or adequate solution of the problem with which it deals.

Footnotes

[23] An address delivered to the Philosophical Society of Manchester in February, 1915. Reprinted from *The Monist*, July, 1915.

[24] Cf. especially Samuel Alexander, "The Basis of Realism," *British Academy*, Vol. VI.

[25] "Are Secondary Qualities Independent of Perception?" *Proc. Arist. Soc.*, 1909-10, pp. 191-218.

[26] First dialogue between Hylas and Philonous, *Works* (Fraser's edition 1901). I. p. 384.

[27] This point has been well urged by the American realists.

[28] Cf. T.P. Nunn, "Are Secondary Qualities Independent of Perception?" *Proc. Arist. Soc.*, 1909-1910.

<

div class="footnote">
9 10 11 12

9.
10.
11.
12.

Chapter **8**

The Relation of Sense-Data to Physics

I. The Problem Stated

Physics is said to be an empirical science, based upon observation and experiment.

It is supposed to be verifiable, i.e. capable of calculating beforehand results subsequently confirmed by observation and experiment.

What can we learn by observation and experiment?

Nothing, so far as physics is concerned, except immediate data of sense: certain patches of colour, sounds, tastes, smells, etc., with certain spatio-temporal relations.

The supposed contents of the physical world are *prima facie* very different from these: molecules have no colour, atoms make no noise, electrons have no taste, and corpuscles do not even smell.

If such objects are to be verified, it must be solely through their relation to sense-data: they must have some kind of correlation with sense-data, and must be verifiable through their correlation *alone*.

But how is the correlation itself ascertained? A correlation can only be ascertained empirically by the correlated objects being constantly *found* together. But in our case, only one term of the correlation, namely, the sensible term, is ever *found*: the other term seems essentially incapable of being found. Therefore, it would seem, the correlation with objects of sense, by which physics was to be verified, is itself utterly and for ever unverifiable.

There are two ways of avoiding this result.

(1) We may say that we know some principle *a priori*, without the need of empirical verification, e.g. that our sense-data have *causes* other than themselves, and that something can be

known about these causes by inference from their effects. This way has been often adopted by philosophers. It may be necessary to adopt this way to some extent, but in so far as it is adopted physics ceases to be empirical or based upon experiment and observation alone. Therefore this way is to be avoided as much as possible.

(2) We may succeed in actually defining the objects of physics as functions of sense-data. Just in so far as physics leads to expectations, this *must* be possible, since we can only *expect* what can be experienced. And in so far as the physical state of affairs is inferred from sense-data, it must be capable of expression as a function of sense-data. The problem of accomplishing this expression leads to much interesting logico-mathematical work.

In physics as commonly set forth, sense-data appear as functions of physical objects: when such-and-such waves impinge upon the eye, we see such-and-such colours, and so on. But the waves are in fact inferred from the colours, not vice versa. Physics cannot be regarded as validly based upon empirical data until the waves have been expressed as functions of the colours and other sense-data.

Thus if physics is to be verifiable we are faced with the following problem: Physics exhibits sense-data as functions of physical objects, but verification is only possible if physical objects can be exhibited as functions of sense-data. We have therefore to solve the equations giving sense-data in terms of physical objects, so as to make them instead give physical objects in terms of sense-data.

II. Characteristics of Sense-Data

When I speak of a "sense-datum," I do not mean the whole of what is given in sense at one time. I mean rather such a part of the whole as might be singled out by attention: particular patches of colour, particular noises, and so on. There is some difficulty in deciding what is to be considered *one* sense-datum: often attention causes divisions to appear where, so far as can be discovered, there were no divisions before. An observed complex fact, such as that this patch of red is to the left of that patch of blue, is also to be regarded as a datum from our present point of view: epistemologically, it does not differ greatly from a simple sense-datum as regards its function in giving knowledge. Its *logical* structure is very different, however, from that of sense: *sense* gives acquaintance with particulars, and is thus a two-term relation in which the object can be *named* but not *asserted*, and is inherently incapable of truth or falsehood, whereas the observation of a complex fact, which may be suitably called perception, is not a two-term relation, but involves the propositional form on the object-side, and gives knowledge of a truth, not mere acquaintance with a particular. This logical difference, important as it is, is not very relevant to our present problem; and it will be convenient to regard data of perception as included among sense-data for the purposes of this paper. It is to be observed that the particulars which are constituents of a datum of perception are always sense-data in the strict sense.

Concerning sense-data, we know that they are there while they are data, and this is the epistemological basis of all our knowledge of external particulars. (The meaning of the word "external" of course raises problems which will concern us later.) We do not know, except by means of more or less precarious inferences, whether the objects which are at one time sense-data continue to exist at times when they are not data. Sense-data at the times when they are data are all that we directly and primitively know of the external world; hence in epistemology the fact that they are *data* is all-important. But the fact that they are all that we directly know gives, of course, no presumption that they are all that there is. If we could construct an impersonal metaphysic, independent of the accidents of our knowledge and ignorance, the privileged position of the actual data would probably disappear, and they would probably appear as a rather haphazard selection from a mass of objects more or less like them. In saying this, I assume only that it is probable that there are particulars with which we are not acquainted. Thus the special importance of sense-data is in relation to epistemology, not to metaphysics. In this respect, physics is to be reckoned as metaphysics: it is impersonal, and nominally pays no special attention to sense-data. It is only when we ask how physics can be *known* that the importance of sense-data re-emerges.

III. Sensibilia

I shall give the name *sensibilia* to those objects which have the same metaphysical and physical status as sense-data, without necessarily being data to any mind. Thus the relation of a *sensibile* to a sense-datum is like that of a man to a husband: a man becomes a husband by entering into the relation of marriage, and similarly a *sensibile* becomes a sense-datum by entering into the relation of acquaintance. It is important to have both terms; for we wish to discuss whether an object which is at one time a sense-datum can still exist at a time when it is not a sense-datum. We cannot ask "Can sense-data exist without being given?" for that is like asking "Can husbands exist without being married?" We must ask "Can *sensibilia* exist without being given?" and also "Can a particular *sensibile* be at one time a sense-datum, and at another not?" Unless we have the word *sensibile* as well as the word "sense-datum," such questions are apt to entangle us in trivial logical puzzles.

It will be seen that all sense-data are *sensibilia*. It is a metaphysical question whether all *sensibilia* are sense-data, and an epistemological question whether there exist means of inferring *sensibilia* which are not data from those that are.

A few preliminary remarks, to be amplified as we proceed, will serve to elucidate the use which I propose to make of *sensibilia*.

I regard sense-data as not mental, and as being, in fact, part of the actual subject-matter of physics. There are arguments, shortly to be examined, for their subjectivity, but these arguments seem to me only to prove *physiological* subjectivity, i.e. causal dependence on the sense-organs, nerves, and brain. The appearance which a thing presents to us is causally dependent upon these, in exactly the same way as it is dependent upon intervening fog or smoke or coloured glass. Both dependences are contained in the statement that the appearance which a piece of matter presents when viewed from a given place is a function not only of the piece of matter, but also of the intervening medium. (The terms used in this statement—"matter," "view from a given place," "appearance," "intervening medium"—will all be defined in the course of the present paper.) We have not the means of ascertaining how things appear from places not surrounded by brain and nerves and sense-organs, because we cannot leave the body; but continuity makes it not unreasonable to suppose that they present *some* appearance at such places. Any such appearance would be included among *sensibilia*. If—*per impossibile*—there were a complete human body with no mind inside it, all those *sensibilia* would exist, in relation to that body, which would be sense-data if there were a mind in the body. What the mind adds to *sensibilia*, in fact, is *merely* awareness: everything else is physical or physiological.

IV. Sense-Data are Physical

Before discussing this question it will be well to define the sense in which the terms "mental" and "physical" are to be used. The word "physical," in all preliminary discussions, is to be understood as meaning "what is dealt with by physics." Physics, it is plain, tells us something about some of the constituents of the actual world; what these constituents are may be doubtful, but it is they that are to be called physical, whatever their nature may prove to be.

The definition of the term "mental" is more difficult, and can only be satisfactorily given after many difficult controversies have been discussed and decided. For present purposes therefore I must content myself with assuming a dogmatic answer to these controversies. I shall call a particular "mental" when it is aware of something, and I shall call a fact "mental" when it contains a mental particular as a constituent.

It will be seen that the mental and the physical are not necessarily mutually exclusive, although I know of no reason to suppose that they overlap.

The doubt as to the correctness of our definition of the "mental" is of little importance in our present discussion. For what I am concerned to maintain is that sense-data are physical, and this being granted it is a matter of indifference in our present inquiry whether or not they are also mental. Although I do not hold, with Mach and James and the "new realists," that the difference between the mental and the physical is *merely* one of arrangement, yet what I have to say in the present paper is compatible with their doctrine and might have been reached from their standpoint.

In discussions on sense-data, two questions are commonly confused, namely:

(1) Do sensible objects persist when we are not sensible of them? in other words, do *sensibilia* which are data at a certain time sometimes continue to exist at times when they are not data? And (2) are sense-data mental or physical?

I propose to assert that sense-data are physical, while yet maintaining that they probably never persist unchanged after ceasing to be data. The view that they do not persist is often thought, quite erroneously in my opinion, to imply that they are mental; and this has, I believe, been a potent source of confusion in regard to our present problem. If there were, as some have held, a *logical impossibility* in sense-data persisting after ceasing to be data, that certainly would tend to show that they were mental; but if, as I contend, their non-persistence is merely a probable inference from empirically ascertained causal laws, then it carries no such implication with it, and we are quite free to treat them as part of the subject-matter of physics.

Logically a sense-datum is an object, a particular of which the subject is aware. It does not contain the subject as a part, as for example beliefs and volitions do. The existence of the sense-datum is therefore not logically dependent upon that of the subject; for the only way, so far as I know, in which the existence of A can be *logically* dependent upon the existence of B is when B is part of A. There is therefore no *a priori* reason why a particular which is a sense-datum should not persist after it has ceased to be a datum, nor why other similar particulars should not exist without ever being data. The view that sense-data are mental is derived, no doubt, in part from their physiological subjectivity, but in part also from a failure to distinguish between sense-data and "sensations." By a sensation I mean the fact consisting in the subject's awareness of the sense-datum. Thus a sensation is a complex of which the subject is a constituent and which therefore is mental. The sense-datum, on the other hand, stands over against the subject as that external object of which in sensation the subject is aware. It is true that the sense-datum is in many cases in the subject's body, but the subject's body is as distinct from the subject as tables and chairs are, and is in fact merely a part of the material world. So soon, therefore, as sense-data are clearly distinguished from sensations, and as their subjectivity is recognised to be physiological not psychical, the chief obstacles in the way of regarding them as physical are removed.

V. "Sensibilia" and "Things"

But if "sensibilia" are to be recognised as the ultimate constituents of the physical world, a long and difficult journey is to be performed before we can arrive either at the "thing" of common sense or at the "matter" of physics. The supposed impossibility of combining the different sense-data which are regarded as appearances of the same "thing" to different people has made it seem as though these "sensibilia" must be regarded as mere subjective phantasms. A given table will present to one man a rectangular appearance, while to another it appears to have two acute angles and two obtuse angles; to one man it appears brown, while to another, towards whom it reflects the light, it appears white and shiny. It is said, not wholly without plausibility, that these different shapes and different colours cannot co-exist simultaneously in the same place, and cannot therefore both be constituents of the physical world. This argument I must confess appeared to me until recently to be irrefutable. The contrary opinion has, however, been ably maintained by Dr. T.P. Nunn in an article entitled: "Are Secondary Qualities Independent of Perception?"[29] The supposed impossibility derives its apparent force from the phrase: "*in the same place*," and it is precisely in this phrase that its weakness lies. The conception of space is too often treated in philosophy—even by those who on reflection would not defend such treatment—as though it were as given, simple, and unambiguous as Kant, in his psychological innocence, supposed. It is the unperceived ambiguity of the word "place" which, as we shall shortly see, has caused the difficulties to realists and given an undeserved advantage to their opponents. Two "places" of different kinds are involved in every sense-datum, namely the place *at* which it appears and the place *from* which it appears. These belong to different spaces, although, as we shall see, it is possible, with certain limitations, to establish a correlation between them. What we call the different appearances of the same thing to different observers are each in a space private to the observer concerned. No place in the private world of one observer is identical with a place in the private world of another observer. There is therefore no question of combining the different appearances in the one place; and the fact that they cannot all exist in one place affords accordingly no ground whatever for questioning their physical reality. The "thing" of common sense may in fact be identified with the whole class of its appearances—where, however, we must include among appearances not only those which are actual sense-data, but also those "sensibilia," if any, which, on grounds of continuity and resemblance, are to be regarded as belonging to the same system of appearances, although there happen to be no observers to whom they are data.

An example may make this clearer. Suppose there are a number of people in a room, all seeing, as they say, the same tables and chairs, walls and pictures. No two of these people have exactly the same sense-data, yet there is sufficient similarity among their data to enable them to group together certain of these data as appearances of one "thing" to the several spectators, and others as appearances of another "thing." Besides the appearances which a given thing in the room presents to the actual spectators, there are, we may suppose, other appearances which it would present to other possible spectators. If a man were to sit down between two others, the appearance which the room would present to him would be intermediate between the appearances which it presents to the two others: and although this appearance would not exist as it is without the sense organs, nerves and brain, of the newly arrived spectator, still it is not unnatural to suppose that, from the position which he now occupies, *some* appearance of the room existed before his arrival. This supposition, however, need merely be noticed and not insisted upon.

Since the "thing" cannot, without indefensible partiality, be identified with any single one of its appearances, it came to be thought of as something distinct from all of them and underlying them. But by the principle of Occam's razor, if the class of appearances will fulfil the purposes for the sake of which the thing was invented by the prehistoric metaphysicians to whom common sense is due, economy demands that we should identify the thing with the class of its appearances. It is not necessary to *deny* a substance or substratum underlying these appearances; it is merely expedient to abstain from asserting this unnecessary entity. Our procedure here is precisely analogous to that which has swept away from the philosophy of mathematics the useless menagerie of metaphysical monsters with which it used to be infested.

VI. Constructions vs. Inferences

Before proceeding to analyse and explain the ambiguities of the word "place," a few general remarks on method are desirable. The supreme maxim in scientific philosophising is this:

<
div class="block">
Wherever possible, logical constructions are to be substituted for inferred entities.

Some examples of the substitution of construction for inference in the realm of mathematical philosophy may serve to elucidate the uses of this maxim. Take first the case of irrationals. In old days, irrationals were inferred as the supposed limits of series of rationals which had no rational limit; but the objection to this procedure was that it left the existence of irrationals merely optative, and for this reason the stricter methods of the present day no longer tolerate such a definition. We now define an irrational number as a certain class of ratios, thus constructing it logically by means of ratios, instead of arriving at it by a doubtful inference from them. Take again the case of cardinal numbers. Two equally numerous collections appear to have something in common: this something is supposed to be their cardinal number. But so long as the cardinal number is inferred from the collections, not constructed in terms of them, its existence must remain in doubt, unless in virtue of a metaphysical postulate *ad hoc*. By defining the cardinal number of a given collection as the class of all equally numerous collections, we avoid the necessity of this metaphysical postulate, and thereby remove a needless element of doubt from the philosophy of arithmetic. A similar method, as I have shown elsewhere, can be applied to classes themselves, which need not be supposed to have any metaphysical reality, but can be regarded as symbolically constructed fictions.

The method by which the construction proceeds is closely analogous in these and all similar cases. Given a set of propositions nominally dealing with the supposed inferred entities, we observe the properties which are required of the supposed entities in order to make these propositions true. By dint of a little logical ingenuity, we then construct some logical function of less hypothetical entities which has the requisite properties.

This constructed function we substitute for the supposed inferred entities, and thereby obtain a new and less doubtful interpretation of the body of propositions in question This method, so fruitful in the philosophy of mathematics, will be found equally applicable in the philosophy of physics, where, I do not doubt, it would have been applied long ago but for the fact that all who have studied this subject hitherto have been completely ignorant of mathematical logic. I myself cannot claim originality in the application of this method to physics, since I owe the suggestion and the stimulus for its application entirely to my friend and collaborator Dr. Whitehead, who is engaged in applying it to the more mathematical portions of the region intermediate between sense-data and the points, instants and particles of physics.

A complete application of the method which substitutes constructions for inferences would exhibit matter wholly in terms of sense-data, and even, we may add, of the sense-data of a single person, since the sense-data of others cannot be known without some element of inference. This, however, must remain for the present an ideal, to be approached as nearly as possible, but to be reached, if at all, only after a long preliminary labour of which as yet we can only see the very beginning. The inferences which are unavoidable can, however, be subjected to certain guiding principles. In the first place they should always be made perfectly explicit, and should be formulated in the most general manner possible. In the second place the inferred entities should, whenever this can be done, be similar to those whose existence is given, rather than, like the Kantian *Ding an sich*, something wholly remote from the data which nominally support the inference. The inferred entities which I shall allow myself are of two kinds: (*a*) the sense-data of other people, in favour of which there is the evidence of testimony, resting ultimately upon the analogical argument in favour of minds other than my own; (*b*) the "sensibilia" which would appear from places where there happen to be no minds, and which I suppose to be real although they are no one's data. Of these two classes of inferred entities, the first will probably be allowed to pass unchallenged. It would give me the greatest satisfaction to be able to dispense with it, and thus establish physics upon a solipsistic basis; but those—and I fear they are the majority—in whom the human affections are stronger than the desire for logical economy, will, no doubt, not share my desire to render solipsism scientifically satisfactory. The second class of inferred entities raises much more serious questions. It may be thought monstrous to maintain that a thing can present any appearance at all in a place where no sense organs and nervous structure exist through which it could appear. I do not myself feel the monstrosity; nevertheless I should regard these supposed appearances only in the light of a hypothetical scaffolding, to be used while the edifice of physics is being raised, though possibly capable of being removed as soon as the edifice is completed. These "sensibilia" which are not data to anyone are therefore to be taken rather as an illustrative hypothesis and as an aid in preliminary statement than as a dogmatic part of the philosophy of physics in its final form.

VII. Private Space and the Space of Perspectives

We have now to explain the ambiguity in the word "place," and how it comes that two places of different sorts are associated with every sense-datum, namely the place *at* which it is and the place *from* which it is perceived. The theory to be advocated is closely analogous to Leibniz's monadology, from which it differs chiefly in being less smooth and tidy.

The first fact to notice is that, so far as can be discovered, no sensibile is ever a datum to two people at [159]once. The things seen by two different people are often closely similar, so similar that the same *words* can be used to denote them, without which communication with others concerning sensible objects would be impossible. But, in spite of this similarity, it would seem that some difference always arises from difference in the point of view. Thus each person, so far as his sense-data are concerned, lives in a private world. This private world contains its own space, or rather spaces, for it would seem that only experience teaches us to correlate the space of sight with the space of touch and with the various other spaces of other senses. This multiplicity of private spaces, however, though interesting to the psychologist, is of no great importance in regard to our present problem, since a merely solipsistic experience enables us to correlate them into the one private space which embraces all our own sense-data. The place *at* which a sense-datum is, is a place in private space. This place therefore is different from any place in the private space of another percipient. For if we assume, as logical economy demands, that all position is relative, a place is only definable by the things in or around it, and therefore the same place cannot occur in two private worlds which have no common constituent. The question, therefore, of combining what we call different appearances of the same thing in the same place does not arise, and the fact that a given object appears to different spectators to have different shapes and colours affords no argument against the physical reality of all these shapes and colours.

In addition to the private spaces belonging to the private worlds of different percipients, there is, however, another space, in which one whole private world counts as a point, or at least as a spatial unit. This might be described as the space of points of view, since each private world may be regarded as the appearance which the universe presents from a certain point of view. I prefer, however, to speak of it as the space of *perspectives*, in order to obviate the suggestion that a private world is only real when someone views it. And for the same reason, when I wish to speak of a private world without assuming a percipient, I shall call it a "perspective."

We have now to explain how the different perspectives are ordered in one space. This is effected by means of the correlated "sensibilia" which are regarded as the appearances, in different perspectives, of one and the same thing. By moving, and by testimony, we discover that two different perspectives, though they cannot both contain the same "sensibilia," may nevertheless contain very similar ones; and the spatial order of a certain group of "sensibilia" in a private space of one perspective is found to be identical with, or very similar to, the spatial order of the correlated "sensibilia" in the private space of another perspective. In this way one "sensibile" in one perspective is correlated with one "sensibile" in another. Such correlated "sensibilia" will be called "appearances of one thing." In Leibniz's monadology, since each monad mirrored the whole universe, there was in each perspective a "sensibile" which was an appearance of each thing. In our system of perspectives, we make no such assumption of completeness. A given thing will have appearances in some perspectives, but presumably not in certain others. The "thing" being defined as the class of its appearances, if κ is the class of perspectives in which a certain thing θ appears, then θ is a member of the multiplicative class of κ, κ being a class of mutually exclusive classes of "sensibilia." And similarly a perspective is a member of the multiplicative class of the things which appear in it.

The arrangement of perspectives in a space is effected by means of the differences between the appearances of a given thing in the various perspectives. Suppose, say, that a certain penny appears in a number of different perspectives; in some it looks larger and in some smaller, in some it looks circular, in others it presents the appearance of an ellipse of varying eccentricity. We may collect together all those perspectives in which the appearance of the penny is circular. These we will place on one straight line, ordering them in a series by the variations in the apparent size of the penny. Those perspectives in which the penny appears as a straight line of a certain thickness will similarly be placed upon a plane (though in this case there will be many different perspectives in which the penny is of the same size; when one arrangement is completed these will form a circle concentric with the penny), and ordered as before by the apparent size of the penny. By such means, all those perspectives in which the penny presents a visual appearance can be arranged in a three-dimensional spatial order. Experience shows that the same spatial order of perspectives would have resulted if, instead of the penny, we had chosen any other thing which appeared in all the perspectives in question, or any other method of utilising the differences between the appearances of the same things in different perspectives. It is this empirical fact which has made it possible to construct the one all-embracing space of physics.

The space whose construction has just been explained, and whose elements are whole perspectives, will be called "perspective-space."

VIII. The Placing of "Things" and "Sensibilia" in Perspective Space

The world which we have so far constructed is a world of six dimensions, since it is a three-dimensional series of perspectives, each of which is itself three-dimensional. We have now to explain the correlation between the perspective space and the various private spaces contained within the various perspectives severally. It is by means of this correlation that the one three-dimensional space of physics is constructed; and it is because of the unconscious performance of this correlation that the distinction between perspective space and the percipient's private space has been blurred, with disastrous results for the philosophy of physics. Let us revert to our penny: the perspectives in which the penny appears larger are regarded as being nearer to the penny than those in which it appears smaller, but as far as experience goes the apparent size of the penny will not grow beyond a certain limit, namely, that where (as we say) the penny is so near the eye that if it were any nearer it could not be seen. By touch we may prolong the series until the penny touches the eye, but no further. If we have been travelling along a line of perspectives in the previously defined sense, we may, however, by imagining the penny removed, prolong the line of perspectives by means, say, of another penny; and the same may be done with any other line of perspectives defined by means of the penny. All these lines meet in a certain place, that is, in a certain perspective. This perspective will be defined as "the place where the penny is."

It is now evident in what sense two places in constructed physical space are associated with a given "sensibile." There is first the place which is the perspective of which the "sensibile" is a member. This is the place *from* which the "sensibile" appears. Secondly there is the place where the thing is of which the "sensibile" is a member, in other words an appearance; this is the place *at* which the "sensibile" appears. The "sensibile" which is a member of one perspective is correlated with another perspective, namely, that which is the place where the thing is of which the "sensibile" is an appearance. To the psychologist the "place from which" is the more interesting, and the "sensibile" accordingly appears to him subjective and where the percipient is. To the physicist the "place at which" is the more interesting, and the "sensibile" accordingly appears to him physical and external. The causes, limits and partial justification of each of these two apparently incompatible views are evident from the above duplicity of places associated with a given "sensibile."

We have seen that we can assign to a physical thing a place in the perspective space. In this way different parts of our body acquire positions in perspective space, and therefore there is a meaning (whether true or false need not much concern us) in saying that the perspective to which our sense-data belong is inside our head. Since our mind is correlated with the perspective to which our sense-data belong, we may regard this perspective as being the position of our mind in perspective space. If, therefore, this perspective is, in the above defined sense, inside our head, there is a good meaning for the statement that the mind is in the head. We can now say of the various appearances of a given thing that some of them are nearer to the thing than others; those are nearer which belong to perspectives that are nearer to "the place where the thing is." We can thus find a meaning, true or false, for the statement that more is to be learnt about a thing by examining it close to than by viewing it from a distance. We can also find a meaning for the phrase "the things which intervene between the subject and a thing of which an appearance is a datum to him." One reason often alleged for the subjectivity of sense-data is that the appearance of a thing may change when we find it hard to suppose that the thing itself has changed—for example, when the change is due to our shutting our eyes, or to our screwing them up so as to make the thing look double. If the thing is defined as the class of its appearances (which is the definition adopted above), there is of course necessarily *some* change in the thing whenever any one of its appearances changes. Nevertheless there is a very important distinction between two different ways in which the appearances may change. If after looking at a thing I shut my eyes, the appearance of my eyes changes in every perspective in which there is such an appearance, whereas most of the appearances of the thing will remain unchanged. We may say, as a matter of definition, that a thing changes when, however near to the thing an appearance of it may be, there are changes in appearances as near as, or still nearer to, the thing. On the other hand we shall say that the change is in some other thing if all appearances of the thing which are at not more than a certain distance from the thing remain unchanged, while only comparatively distant appearances of the thing are altered. From this consideration we are naturally led to the consideration of *matter*, which must be our next topic.

IX. The Definition of Matter

We defined the "physical thing" as the class of its appearances, but this can hardly be taken as a definition of matter. We want to be able to express the fact that the appearance of a thing in a given perspective is causally affected by the matter between the thing and the perspective. We have found a meaning for "between a thing and a perspective." But we want matter to be something other than the whole class of appearances of a thing, in order to state the influence of matter on appearances.

We commonly assume that the information we get about a thing is more accurate when the thing is nearer. Far off, we see it is a man; then we see it is Jones; then we see he is smiling. Complete accuracy would only be attainable as a limit: if the appearances of Jones as we approach him tend towards a limit, that limit may be taken to be what Jones really is. It is obvious that from the point of view of physics the appearances of a thing close to "count" more than the appearances far off. We may therefore set up the following tentative definition:

The *matter* of a given thing is the limit of its appearances as their distance from the thing diminishes.

It seems probable that there is something in this definition, but it is not quite satisfactory, because empirically there is no such limit to be obtained from sense-data. The definition will have to be eked out by constructions and definitions. But probably it suggests the right direction in which to look.

We are now in a position to understand in outline the reverse journey from matter to sense-data which is performed by physics. The appearance of a thing in a given perspective is a function of the matter composing the thing and of the intervening matter. The appearance of a thing is altered by intervening smoke or mist, by blue spectacles or by alterations in the sense-organs or nerves of the percipient (which also must be reckoned as part of the intervening medium). The nearer we approach to the thing, the less its appearance is affected by the intervening matter. As we travel further and further from the thing, its appearances diverge more and more from their initial character; and the causal laws of their divergence are to be stated in terms of the matter which lies between them and the thing. Since the appearances at very small distances are less affected by causes other than the thing itself, we come to think that the limit towards which these appearances tend as the distance diminishes is what the thing "really is," as opposed to what it merely seems to be. This, together with its necessity for the statement of causal laws, seems to be the source of the entirely erroneous feeling that matter is more "real" than sense-data.

Consider for example the infinite divisibility of matter. In looking at a given thing and approaching it, one sense-datum will become several, and each of these will again divide. Thus *one* appearance may represent *many* things, and to this process there seems no end. Hence in the limit, when we approach indefinitely near to the thing there will be an indefinite number of units of matter corresponding to what, at a finite distance, is only one appearance. This is how infinite divisibility arises.

The whole causal efficacy of a thing resides in its matter. This is in some sense an empirical fact, but it would be hard to state it precisely, because "causal efficacy" is difficult to define.

What can be known empirically about the matter of a thing is only approximate, because we cannot get to know the appearances of the thing from very small distances, and cannot accurately infer the limit of these appearances. But it *is* inferred *approximately* by means of the appearances we can observe. It then turns out that these appearances can be exhibited by physics as a function of the matter in our immediate neighbourhood; e.g. the visual appearance of a distant object is a function of the light-waves that reach the eyes. This leads to confusions of thought, but offers no real difficulty.

One appearance, of a visible object for example, is not sufficient to determine its other simultaneous appearances, although it goes a certain distance towards determining them. The determination of the hidden structure of a thing, so far as it is possible at all, can only be effected by means of elaborate dynamical inferences.

X. Time

[30]

It seems that the one all-embracing time is a construction, like the one all-embracing space. Physics itself has become conscious of this fact through the discussions connected with relativity.

Between two perspectives which both belong to one person's experience, there will be a direct time-relation of before and after. This suggests a way of dividing history in the same sort of way as it is divided by different experiences, but without introducing experience or any thing mental: we may define a "biography" as everything that is (directly) earlier or later than, or simultaneous with, a given "sensibile." This will give a series of perspectives, which *might* all form parts of one person's experience, though it is not necessary that all or any of them should actually do so. By this means, the history of the world is divided into a number of mutually exclusive biographies.

We have now to correlate the times in the different biographies. The natural thing would be to say that the appearances of a given (momentary) thing in two different perspectives belonging to different biographies are to be taken as simultaneous; but this is not convenient. Suppose *A* shouts to *B*, and *B* replies as soon as he hears *A's* shout. Then between *A's* hearing of his own shout and his hearing of *B's* there is an interval; thus if we made *A's* and *B's* hearing of the same shout exactly simultaneous with each other, we should have events exactly simultaneous with a given event but not with each other. To obviate this, we assume a "velocity of sound." That is, we assume that the time when *B* hears *A's* shout is half-way between the time when *A* hears his own shout and the time when he hears *B's*. In this way the correlation is effected.

What has been said about sound applies of course equally to light. The general principle is that the appearances, in different perspectives, which are to be grouped together as constituting what a certain thing is at a certain moment, are not to be all regarded as being at that moment. On the contrary they spread outward from the thing with various velocities according to the nature of the appearances. Since no *direct* means exist of correlating the time in one biography with the time in another, this temporal grouping of the appearances belonging to a given thing at a given moment is in part conventional. Its motive is partly to secure the verification of such maxims as that events which are exactly simultaneous with the same event are exactly simultaneous with one another, partly to secure convenience in the formulation of causal laws.

XI. The Persistence of Things and Matter

Apart from any of the fluctuating hypotheses of physics, three main problems arise in connecting the world of physics with the world of sense, namely:

1. the construction of a single space;
2. the construction of a single time;
3. the construction of permanent things or matter.

We have already considered the first and second of these problems; it remains to consider the third.

We have seen how correlated appearances in different perspectives are combined to form one "thing" at one moment in the all-embracing time of physics. We have now to consider how appearances at different times are combined as belonging to one "thing," and how we arrive at the persistent "matter" of physics. The assumption of permanent substance, which technically underlies the procedure of physics, cannot of course be regarded as metaphysically legitimate: just as the one thing simultaneously seen by many people is a construction, so the one thing seen at different times by the same or different people must be a construction, being in fact nothing but a certain grouping of certain "sensibilia."

We have seen that the momentary state of a "thing" is an assemblage of "sensibilia," in different perspectives, not all simultaneous in the one constructed time, but spreading out from "the place where the thing is" with velocities depending upon the nature of the "sensibilia." The time *at* which the "thing" is in this state is the lower limit of the times at which these appearances occur. We have now to consider what leads us to speak of another set of appearances as belonging to the same "thing" at a different time.

For this purpose, we may, at least to begin with, confine ourselves within a single biography. If we can always say when two "sensibilia" in a given biography are appearances of one thing, then, since we have seen how to connect "sensibilia" in different biographies as appearances of the same momentary state of a thing, we shall have all that is necessary for the complete construction of the history of a thing.

It is to be observed, to begin with, that the identity of a thing for common sense is not always correlated with the identity of matter for physics. A human body is one persisting thing for common sense, but for physics its matter is constantly changing. We may say, broadly, that the common-sense conception is based upon continuity in appearances at the ordinary distances of sense-data, while the physical conception is based upon the continuity of appearances at very small distances from the thing. It is probable that the common-sense conception is not capable of complete precision. Let us therefore concentrate our attention upon the conception of the persistence of matter in physics.

The first characteristic of two appearances of the same piece of matter at different times is *continuity*. The two appearances must be connected by a series of intermediaries, which, if time and space form compact series, must themselves form a compact series. The colour of the leaves is different in autumn from what it is in summer; but we believe that the change occurs gradually, and that, if the colours are different at two given times, there are intermediate times at which the colours are intermediate between those at the given times.

But there are two considerations that are important as regards continuity.

First, it is largely hypothetical. We do not observe any one thing continuously, and it is merely a hypothesis to assume that, while we are not observing it, it passes through conditions intermediate between those in which it is perceived. During uninterrupted observation, it is true, continuity is nearly verified; but even here, when motions are very rapid, as in the case of explosions, the continuity is not actually capable of direct verification. Thus we can only say that the sense-data are found to *permit* a hypothetical complement of "sensibilia" such as will preserve continuity, and that therefore there *may* be such a complement. Since, however, we have already made such use of hypothetical "sensibilia," we will let this point pass, and admit such "sensibilia," as are required to preserve continuity.

Secondly, continuity is not a sufficient criterion of material identity. It is true that in many cases, such as rocks, mountains, tables, chairs, etc., where the appearances change slowly, continuity is sufficient, but in other cases, such as the parts of an approximately homogeneous fluid, it fails us utterly. We can travel by sensibly continuous gradations from any one drop of the sea at any one time to any other drop at any other time. We infer the motions of sea-water from the effects of the current, but they cannot be inferred from direct sensible observation together with the assumption of continuity.

The characteristic required in addition to continuity is conformity with the laws of dynamics. Starting from what common sense regards as persistent things, and making only such modifications as from time to time seem reasonable, we arrive at assemblages of "sensibilia" which are found to obey certain simple laws, namely those of dynamics. By regarding "sensibilia" at different times as belonging to the same piece of matter, we are able to define *motion*, which presupposes the assumption or construction of something persisting throughout the time of the motion. The motions which are regarded as occurring, during a period in which all the "sensibilia" and the times of their appearance are given, will be different according to the manner in which we combine "sensibilia" at different times as belonging to the same piece of matter. Thus even when the whole history of the world is given in every particular, the question what motions take place is still to a certain extent arbitrary even after the assumption of continuity. Experience shows that it is possible to determine motions in such a way as to satisfy the laws of dynamics, and that this determination, roughly and on the whole, is fairly in agreement with the common-sense opinions about persistent things. This determination, therefore, is adopted, and leads to a criterion by which we can determine, sometimes practically, sometimes only theoretically, whether two appearances at different times are to be regarded as belonging to the same piece of matter. The persistence of all matter throughout all time can, I imagine, be secured by definition.

To recommend this conclusion, we must consider what it is that is proved by the empirical success of physics. What is proved is that its hypotheses, though unverifiable where they go beyond sense-data, are at no point in contradiction with sense-data, but, on the contrary, are ideally such as to render all sense-data calculable when a sufficient collection of "sensibilia" is given. Now physics has found it empirically possible to collect sense-data into series, each series being regarded as belonging to one "thing," and behaving, with regard to the laws of physics, in a way in which series not belonging to one thing would in general not behave. If it is to be unambiguous whether two appearances belong to the same thing or not, there must be only one way of grouping appearances so that the resulting things obey the laws of physics. It would be very difficult to prove that this is the case, but for our present purposes we may let this point pass, and assume that there is only one way. Thus we may lay down the following definition: *Physical things are those series of appearances whose matter obeys the laws of physics*. That such series exist is an empirical fact, which constitutes the verifiability of physics.

XII. Illusions, Hallucinations, and Dreams

It remains to ask how, in our system, we are to find a place for sense-data which apparently fail to have the usual connection with the world of physics. Such sense-data are of various kinds, requiring somewhat different treatment. But all are of the sort that would be called "unreal," and therefore, before embarking upon the discussion, certain logical remarks must be made upon the conceptions of reality and unreality.

Mr. A. Wolf[31] says:

<

div class="block">

"The conception of mind as a system of transparent activities is, I think, also untenable because of its failure to account for the very possibility of dreams and hallucinations. It seems impossible to realise how a bare, transparent activity can be directed to what is not there, to apprehend what is not given."

This statement is one which, probably, most people would endorse. But it is open to two objections. First it is difficult to see how an activity, however un-"transparent," can be directed towards a nothing: a term of a relation cannot be a mere nonentity. Secondly, no reason is given, and I am convinced that none can be given, for the assertion that dream-objects are not "there" and not "given." Let us take the second point first.

(1) The belief that dream-objects are not given comes, I think, from failure to distinguish, as regards waking life, between the sense-datum and the corresponding "thing." In dreams, there is no such corresponding "thing" as the dreamer supposes; if, therefore, the "thing" were given in waking life, as e.g. Meinong maintains,[32] then there would be a difference in respect of givenness between dreams and waking life. But if, as we have maintained, what is given is never the thing, but merely one of the "sensibilia" which compose the thing, then what we apprehend in a dream is just as much given as what we apprehend in waking life.

Exactly the same argument applies as to the dream-objects being "there." They have their position in the private space of the perspective of the dreamer; where they fail is in their correlation with other private spaces and therefore with perspective space. But in the only sense in which "there" can be a datum, they are "there" just as truly as any of the sense-data of waking life.

(2) The conception of "illusion" or "unreality," and the correlative conception of "reality," are generally used in a way which embodies profound logical confusions. Words that go in pairs, such as "real" and "unreal," "existent" and "non-existent," "valid" and "invalid," etc., are all derived from the one fundamental pair, "true" and "false." Now "true" and "false" are applicable only—except in derivative significations—to *propositions*. Thus wherever the above pairs can be significantly applied, we must be dealing either with propositions or with such incomplete phrases as only acquire meaning when put into a context which, with them, forms a proposition. Thus such pairs of words can be applied to *descriptions*,[33] but not to proper names: in other words, they have no application whatever to data, but only to entities or non-entities described in terms of data.

Let us illustrate by the terms "existence" and "non-existence." Given any datum x, it is meaningless either to assert or to deny that x "exists." We might be tempted to say: "Of course x exists, for otherwise it could not be a datum." But such a statement is really meaningless, although it is significant and true to say "My present sense-datum exists," and it may also be true that "x is my present sense-datum." The inference from these two propositions to "x exists" is one which seems irresistible to people unaccustomed to logic; yet the apparent proposition inferred is not merely false, but strictly meaningless. To say "My present sense-datum exists" is to say (roughly): "There is an object of which 'my present sense-datum' is a description." But we cannot say: "There is an object of which 'x' is a description," because 'x' is (in the case we are supposing) a name, not a description. Dr. Whitehead and I have explained this point fully elsewhere (*loc. cit.*) with the help of symbols, without which it is hard to understand; I shall not therefore here repeat the demonstration of the above propositions, but shall proceed with their application to our present problem.

The fact that "existence" is only applicable to descriptions is concealed by the use of what are grammatically proper names in a way which really transforms them into descriptions. It is, for example, a legitimate question whether Homer existed; but here "Homer" means "the author of the Homeric poems," and is a description. Similarly we may ask whether God exists; but then "God" means "the Supreme Being" or "the *ens realissimum*" or whatever other description we may prefer. If "God" were a proper name, God would have to be a datum; and then no question could arise as to His existence. The distinction between existence and other predicates, which Kant obscurely felt, is brought to light by the theory of descriptions, and is seen to remove "existence" altogether from the fundamental notions of metaphysics.

What has been said about "existence" applies equally to "reality," which may, in fact, be taken as synonymous with "existence." Concerning the immediate objects in illusions, hallucinations, and dreams, it is meaningless to ask whether they "exist" or are "real." There they are, and that ends the matter. But we may legitimately inquire as to the existence or reality of "things" or other "sensibilia" inferred from such objects. It is the unreality of these "things" and other "sensibilia," together with a failure to notice that they are not data, which has led to the view that the objects of dreams are unreal.

We may now apply these considerations in detail to the stock arguments against realism, though what is to be said will be mainly a repetition of what others have said before.

(1) We have first the variety of normal appearances, supposed to be incompatible. This is the case of the different shapes and colours which a given thing presents to different spectators. Locke's water which seems both hot and cold belongs to this class of cases. Our system of different perspectives fully accounts for these cases, and shows that they afford no argument against realism.

(2) We have cases where the correlation between different senses is unusual. The bent stick in water belongs here. People say it looks bent but is straight: this only means that it is straight to the touch, though bent to sight. There is no "illusion," but only a false inference, if we think that the stick would feel bent to the touch. The stick would look just as bent in a photograph, and, as Mr. Gladstone used to say, "the photograph cannot lie."[34] The case of seeing double also belongs here, though in this case the cause of the unusual correlation is physiological, and would therefore not operate in a

photograph. It is a mistake to ask whether the "thing" is duplicated when we see it double. The "thing" is a whole system of "sensibilia," and it is only those visual "sensibilia" which are data to the percipient that are duplicated. The phenomenon has a purely physiological explanation; indeed, in view of our having two eyes, it is in less need of explanation than the single visual sense-datum which we normally obtain from the things on which we focus.

(3) We come now to cases like dreams, which may, at the moment of dreaming, contain nothing to arouse suspicion, but are condemned on the ground of their supposed incompatibility with earlier and later data. Of course it often happens that dream-objects fail to behave in the accustomed manner: heavy objects fly, solid objects melt, babies turn into pigs or undergo even greater changes. But none of these unusual occurrences *need* happen in a dream, and it is not on account of such occurrences that dream-objects are called "unreal." It is their lack of continuity with the dreamer's past and future that makes him, when he wakes, condemn them; and it is their lack of correlation with other private worlds that makes others condemn them. Omitting the latter ground, our reason for condemning them is that the "things" which we infer from them cannot be combined according to the laws of physics with the "things" inferred from waking sense-data. This might be used to condemn the "things" inferred from the data of dreams. Dream-data are no doubt appearances of "things," but not of such "things" as the dreamer supposes. I have no wish to combat psychological theories of dreams, such as those of the psycho-analysts. But there certainly are cases where (whatever psychological causes may contribute) the presence of physical causes also is very evident. For instance, a door banging may produce a dream of a naval engagement, with images of battleships and sea and smoke. The whole dream will be an appearance of the door banging, but owing to the peculiar condition of the body (especially the brain) during sleep, this appearance is not that expected to be produced by a door banging, and thus the dreamer is led to entertain false beliefs. But his sense-data are still physical, and are such as a completed physics would include and calculate.

(4) The last class of illusions are those which cannot be discovered within one person's experience, except through the discovery of discrepancies with the experiences of others. Dreams might conceivably belong to this class, if they were jointed sufficiently neatly into waking life; but the chief instances are recurrent sensory hallucinations of the kind that lead to insanity. What makes the patient, in such cases, become what others call insane is the fact that, within his own experience, there is nothing to show that the hallucinatory sense-data do not have the usual kind of connection with "sensibilia" in other perspectives. Of course he may learn this through testimony, but he probably finds it simpler to suppose that the testimony is untrue and that he is being wilfully deceived. There is, so far as I can see, no theoretical criterion by which the patient can decide, in such a case, between the two equally satisfactory hypotheses of his madness and of his friends' mendacity.

From the above instances it would appear that abnormal sense-data, of the kind which we regard as deceptive, have intrinsically just the same status as any others, but differ as regards their correlations or causal connections with other "sensibilia" and with "things." Since the usual correlations and connections become part of our unreflective expectations, and even seem, except to the psychologist, to form part of our data, it comes to be thought, mistakenly, that in such cases the data are unreal, whereas they are merely the causes of false inferences. The fact that correlations and connections of unusual kinds occur adds to the difficulty of inferring things from sense and of expressing physics in terms of sense-data. But the unusualness would seem to be always physically or physiologically explicable, and therefore raises only a complication, not a philosophical objection.

I conclude, therefore, that no valid objection exists to the view which regards sense-data as part of the actual substance of the physical world, and that, on the other hand, this view is the only one which accounts for the empirical verifiability of physics. In the present paper, I have given only a rough preliminary sketch. In particular, the part played by *time* in the construction of the physical world is, I think, more fundamental than would appear from the above account. I should hope that, with further elaboration, the part played by unperceived "sens-ibilia" could be indefinitely diminished, probably by invoking the history of a "thing" to eke out the inferences derivable from its momentary appearance.

Footnotes

[29] *Proc. Arist. Soc.*, 1909-1910, pp. 191-218.

[30] On this subject, compare *A Theory of Time and Space*, by Mr. A.A. Robb (Camb. Univ. Press), which first suggested to me the views advocated here, though I have, for present purposes, omitted what is most interesting and novel in his theory. Mr. Robb has given a sketch of his theory in a pamphlet with the same title (Heffer and Sons, Cambridge, 1913).

[31] "Natural Realism and Present Tendencies in Philosophy," *Proc. Arist. Soc.*, 1908-1909, p. 165.

[32] *Die Erfahrungsgrundlagen unseres Wissens*, p. 28.

[33] Cf. *Principia Mathematica*, Vol. I, * 14, and Introduction, Chap. III. For the definition of *existence*, cf. * 14. 02.

[34] Cf. Edwin B. Holt, *The Place of Illusory Experience in a Realistic World.* "The New Realism," p. 303, both on this point and as regards *seeing double*.

<
div class="footnote">
13 14 15 16

13.
14.
15.
16.

9

On the Notion of Cause

In the following paper I wish, first, to maintain that the word "cause" is so inextricably bound up with misleading associations as to make its complete extrusion from the philosophical vocabulary desirable; secondly, to inquire what principle, if any, is employed in science in place of the supposed "law of causality" which philosophers imagine to be employed; thirdly, to exhibit certain confusions, especially in regard to teleology and determinism, which appear to me to be connected with erroneous notions as to causality.

All philosophers, of every school, imagine that causation is one of the fundamental axioms or postulates of science, yet, oddly enough, in advanced sciences such as gravitational astronomy, the word "cause" never occurs. Dr. James Ward, in his *Naturalism and Agnosticism*, makes this a ground of complaint against physics: the business of those who wish to ascertain the ultimate truth about the world, he apparently thinks, should be the discovery of causes, yet physics never even seeks them. To me it seems that philosophy ought not to assume such legislative functions, and that the reason why physics has ceased to look for causes is that, in fact, there are no such things. The law of causality, I believe, like much that passes muster among philosophers, is a relic of a bygone age, surviving, like the monarchy, only because it is erroneously supposed to do no harm. In order to find out what philosophers commonly understand by "cause," I consulted Baldwin's *Dictionary*, and was rewarded beyond my expectations, for I found the following three mutually incompatible definitions:—
<
    div class="block3">

"Causality. (1) The necessary connection of events in the time-series... .

"Cause (notion of). Whatever may be included in the thought or perception of a process as taking place in consequence of another process... .

"Cause and Effect. (1) Cause and effect ... are correlative terms denoting any two distinguishable things, phases, or aspects of reality, which are so related to each other that whenever the first ceases to exist the second comes into existence immediately after, and whenever the second comes into existence the first has ceased to exist immediately before."

Let us consider these three definitions in turn. The first, obviously, is unintelligible without a definition of "necessary." Under this head, Baldwin's *Dictionary* gives the following:—
<
div class="block3">
"Necessary. That is necessary which not only is true, but would be true under all circumstances. Something more than brute compulsion is, therefore, involved in the conception; there is a general law under which the thing takes place."

The notion of cause is so intimately connected with that of necessity that it will be no digression to linger over the above definition, with a view to discovering, if possible, *some* meaning of which it is capable; for, as it stands, it is very far from having any definite signification.

The first point to notice is that, if any meaning is to be given to the phrase "would be true under all circumstances," the subject of it must be a propositional function, not a proposition.[35] A proposition is simply true or false, and that ends the matter: there can be no question of "circumstances." "Charles I's head was cut off" is just as true in summer as in winter, on Sundays as on Mondays. Thus when it is worth saying that something "would be true under all circumstances," the something in question must be a propositional function, i.e. an expression containing a variable, and becoming a proposition when a value is assigned to the variable; the varying "circumstances" alluded to are then the different values of which the variable is capable. Thus if "necessary" means "what is true under all circumstances," then "if x is a man, x is mortal" is

necessary, because it is true for any possible value of x. Thus we should be led to the following definition:—
<
  div class="block3">
"Necessary is a predicate of a propositional function, meaning that it is true for all possible values of its argument or arguments."

Unfortunately, however, the definition in Baldwin's *Dictionary* says that what is necessary is not only "true under all circumstances" but is also "true." Now these two are incompatible. Only propositions can be "true," and only propositional functions can be "true under all circumstances." Hence the definition as it stands is nonsense. What is meant seems to be this: "A proposition is necessary when it is a value of a propositional function which is true under all circumstances, i.e. for all values of its argument or arguments." But if we adopt this definition, the same proposition will be necessary or contingent according as we choose one or other of its terms as the argument to our propositional function. For example, "if Socrates is a man, Socrates is mortal," is necessary if Socrates is chosen as argument, but not if *man* or *mortal* is chosen. Again, "if Socrates is a man, Plato is mortal," will be necessary if either Socrates or *man* is chosen as argument, but not if Plato or *mortal* is chosen. However, this difficulty can be overcome by specifying the constituent which is to be regarded as argument, and we thus arrive at the following definition:

"A proposition is *necessary* with respect to a given constituent if it remains true when that constituent is altered in any way compatible with the proposition remaining significant."

We may now apply this definition to the definition of causality quoted above. It is obvious that the argument must be the time at which the earlier event occurs. Thus an instance of causality will be such as: "If the event e_1 occurs at the time t_1, it will be followed by the event e_2." This proposition is intended to be necessary with respect to t_1, i.e. to remain true however t_1 may be varied. Causality, as a universal law, will then be the following: "Given any event e_1, there is an event e_2 such that, whenever e_1 occurs, e_2 occurs later." But before this can be considered precise, we must specify how much later e_2 is to occur. Thus the principle becomes:—

"Given any event e_1, there is an event e_2 and a time-interval τ such that, whenever e_1 occurs, e_2 follows after an interval τ."

I am not concerned as yet to consider whether this law is true or false. For the present, I am merely concerned to discover what the law of causality is supposed to be. I pass, therefore, to the other definitions quoted above.

The second definition need not detain us long, for two reasons. First, because it is psychological: not the "thought or perception" of a process, but the process itself, must be what concerns us in considering causality. Secondly, because it is circular: in speaking of a process as "taking place in consequence of" another process, it introduces the very notion of cause which was to be defined.

The third definition is by far the most precise; indeed as regards clearness it leaves nothing to be desired. But a great difficulty is caused by the temporal contiguity of cause and effect which the definition asserts. No two instants are contiguous, since the time-series is compact; hence either the cause or the effect or both must, if the definition is correct, endure for a finite time; indeed, by the wording of the definition it is plain that both are assumed to endure for a finite time. But then we are faced with a dilemma: if the cause is a process involving change within itself, we shall require (if causality is universal) causal relations between its earlier and later parts; moreover, it would seem that only the later parts can be relevant to the effect, since the earlier parts are not contiguous to the effect, and therefore (by the definition) cannot influence the effect. Thus we shall be led to diminish the duration of the cause without limit, and however much we may diminish it, there will still remain an earlier part which might be altered without altering the effect, so that the true cause, as defined, will not have been reached, for it will be observed that the definition excludes plurality of causes. If, on the other hand, the cause is purely static, involving no change within itself, then, in the first place, no such cause is to be found in nature, and in the second place, it seems strange—too strange to be accepted, in spite of bare logical possibility—that the cause, after existing placidly for some time, should suddenly explode into the effect, when it might just as well have done so at any earlier time, or have gone on unchanged without producing its effect. This dilemma, therefore, is fatal to the view that cause and effect can be contiguous in time; if there are causes and effects, they must be separated by a finite time-interval τ, as was assumed in the above interpretation of the first definition.

What is essentially the same statement of the law of causality as the one elicited above from the first of Baldwin's definitions is given by other philosophers. Thus John Stuart Mill says:—

"The Law of Causation, the recognition of which is the main pillar of inductive science, is but the familiar truth, that invariability of succession is found by observation to obtain between every fact in nature and some other fact which has preceded it."[36]

And Bergson, who has rightly perceived that the law as stated by philosophers is worthless, nevertheless continues to suppose that it is used in science. Thus he says:—

"Now, it is argued, this law [the law of causality] means that every phenomenon is determined by its conditions, or, in other words, that the same causes produce the same effects."[37]

And again:—

"We perceive physical phenomena, and these phenomena obey laws. This means: (1) That phenomena a, b, c, d, previously perceived, can occur again in the same shape; (2) that a certain phenomenon P, which appeared after the conditions a, b, c, d, and after these conditions only, will not fail to recur as soon as the same conditions are again present."[39]

A great part of Bergson's attack on science rests on the assumption that it employs this principle. In fact, it employs no such principle, but philosophers—even Bergson—are too apt to take their views on science from each other, not from science. As to what the principle is, there is a fair consensus among philosophers of different schools. There are, however, a number of difficulties which at once arise. I omit the question of plurality of causes for the present, since other graver questions have to be considered. Two of these, which are forced on our attention by the above statement of the law, are the following:—
<
div class="block">
(1) What is meant by an "event"?

(2) How long may the time-interval be between cause and effect?

(1) An "event," in the statement of the law, is obviously intended to be something that is likely to recur since otherwise the law becomes trivial. It follows that an "event" is not a particular, but some universal of which there may be many instances. It follows also that an "event" must be something short of the whole state of the universe, since it is highly improbable that this will recur. What is meant by an "event" is something like striking a match, or dropping a penny into the slot of an automatic machine. If such an event is to recur, it must not be defined too narrowly: we must not state with what degree of force the match is to be struck, nor what is to be the temperature of the penny. For if such considerations were relevant, our "event" would occur at most once, and the law would cease to give information. An "event," then, is a universal defined sufficiently widely to admit of many particular occurrences in time being instances of it.

(2) The next question concerns the time-interval. Philosophers, no doubt, think of cause and effect as contiguous in time, but this, for reasons already given, is impossible. Hence, since there are no infinitesimal time-intervals, there must be some finite lapse of time τ between cause and effect. This, however, at once raises insuperable difficulties. However short we make the interval τ, something may happen during this interval which prevents the expected result. I put my penny in the slot, but before I can draw out my ticket there is an earthquake which upsets the machine and my calculations. In order to be sure of the expected effect, we must know that there is nothing in the environment to interfere with it. But this means that the supposed cause is not, by itself, adequate to insure the effect. And as soon as we include the environment, the probability of repetition is diminished, until at last, when the whole environment is included, the probability of repetition becomes almost *nil*.

In spite of these difficulties, it must, of course, be admitted that many fairly dependable regularities of sequence occur in daily life. It is these regularities that have suggested the supposed law of causality; where they are found to fail, it is thought that a better formulation could have been found which would have never failed. I am far from denying that there may be such sequences which in fact never do fail. It may be that there will never be an exception to the rule that when a stone of more than a certain mass, moving with more than a certain velocity, comes in contact with a pane of glass of less than a certain thickness, the glass breaks. I also do not deny that the observation of such regularities, even when they are not without exceptions, is useful in the infancy of a science: the observation that unsupported bodies in air usually fall was a stage on the way to the law of gravitation. What I deny is that science assumes the existence of invariable uniformities of sequence of this kind, or that it aims at discovering them. All such uniformities, as we saw, depend upon a certain vagueness in the definition of the "events." That bodies fall is a vague qualitative statement; science wishes to know how fast they fall. This depends upon the shape of the bodies and the density of the air. It is true that there is more nearly uniformity when they fall in a vacuum; so far as Galileo could observe, the uniformity is then complete. But later it appeared that even there the latitude made a difference, and the altitude. Theoretically, the position of the sun and moon must make a difference. In short, every advance in a science takes us farther away from the crude uniformities which are first observed, into greater differentiation of antecedent and consequent, and into a continually wider circle of antecedents recognised as relevant.

The principle "same cause, same effect," which philosophers imagine to be vital to science, is therefore utterly otiose. As soon as the antecedents have been given sufficiently fully to enable the consequent to be calculated with some exactitude, the antecedents have become so complicated that it is very unlikely they will ever recur. Hence, if this were the principle involved, science would remain utterly sterile.

The importance of these considerations lies partly in the fact that they lead to a more correct account of scientific procedure, partly in the fact that they remove the analogy with human volition which makes the conception of cause such a fruitful source of fallacies. The latter point will become clearer by the help of some illustrations. For this purpose I shall consider a few maxims which have played a great part in the history of philosophy.

(1) "Cause and effect must more or less resemble each other." This principle was prominent in the philosophy of occasionalism, and is still by no means extinct. It is still often thought, for example, that mind could not have grown up in a universe which previously contained nothing mental, and one ground for this belief is that matter is too dissimilar from mind to have been able to cause it. Or, more particularly, what are termed the nobler parts of our nature are supposed to be inexplicable, unless the universe always contained something at least equally noble which could cause them. All such views seem to depend upon assuming some unduly simplified law of causality; for, in any legitimate sense of "cause" and "effect," science seems to show that they are usually very widely dissimilar, the "cause" being, in fact, two states of the whole universe, and the "effect" some particular event.

(2) "Cause is analogous to volition, since there must be an intelligible *nexus* between cause and effect." This maxim is, I think, often unconsciously in the imaginations of philosophers who would reject it when explicitly stated. It is probably operative in the view we have just been considering, that mind could not have resulted from a purely material world. I do not profess to know what is meant by "intelligible"; it seems to mean "familiar to imagination." Nothing is less "intelligible," in any other sense, than the connection between an act of will and its fulfilment. But obviously the sort of nexus desired between cause and effect is such as could only hold between the "events" which the supposed law of causality contemplates; the laws which replace causality in such a science as physics leave no room for any two events between which a nexus could be sought.

(3) "The cause *compels* the effect in some sense in which the effect does not compel the cause." This belief seems largely operative in the dislike of determinism; but, as a matter of fact, it is connected with our second maxim, and falls as soon as that is abandoned. We may define "compulsion" as follows: "Any set of circumstances is said to compel A when A desires to do something which the circumstances prevent, or to abstain from something which the circumstances cause." This presupposes that some meaning has been found for the word "cause"—a point to which I shall return later. What I want to make clear at

present is that compulsion is a very complex notion, involving thwarted desire. So long as a person does what he wishes to do, there is no compulsion, however much his wishes may be calculable by the help of earlier events. And where desire does not come in, there can be no question of compulsion. Hence it is, in general, misleading to regard the cause as compelling the effect.

A vaguer form of the same maxim substitutes the word "determine" for the word "compel"; we are told that the cause *determines* the effect in a sense in which the effect does not *determine* the cause. It is not quite clear what is meant by "determining"; the only precise sense, so far as I know, is that of a function or one-many relation. If we admit plurality of causes, but not of effects, that is, if we suppose that, given the cause, the effect must be such and such, but, given the effect, the cause may have been one of many alternatives, then we may say that the cause determines the effect, but not the effect the cause. Plurality of causes, however, results only from conceiving the effect vaguely and narrowly and the cause precisely and widely. Many antecedents may "cause" a man's death, because his death is vague and narrow. But if we adopt the opposite course, taking as the "cause" the drinking of a dose of arsenic, and as the "effect" the whole state of the world five minutes later, we shall have plurality of effects instead of plurality of causes. Thus the supposed lack of symmetry between "cause" and "effect" is illusory.

(4) "A cause cannot operate when it has ceased to exist, because what has ceased to exist is nothing." This is a common maxim, and a still more common unexpressed prejudice. It has, I fancy, a good deal to do with the attractiveness of Bergson's "*durée*": since the past has effects now, it must still exist in some sense. The mistake in this maxim consists in the supposition that causes "operate" at all. A volition "operates" when what it wills takes place; but nothing can operate except a volition. The belief that causes "operate" results from assimilating them, consciously or unconsciously, to volitions. We have already seen that, if there are causes at all, they must be separated by a finite interval of time from their effects, and thus cause their effects after they have ceased to exist.

It may be objected to the above definition of a volition "operating" that it only operates when it "causes" what it wills, not when it merely happens to be followed by what it wills. This certainly represents the usual view of what is meant by a volition "operating," but as it involves the very view of causation which we are engaged in combating, it is not open to us as a definition. We may say that a volition "operates" when there is some law in virtue of which a similar volition in rather similar circumstances will usually be followed by what it wills. But this is a vague conception, and introduces ideas which we have not yet considered. What is chiefly important to notice is that the usual notion of "operating" is not open to us if we reject, as I contend that we should, the usual notion of causation.

(5) "A cause cannot operate except where it is." This maxim is very widespread; it was urged against Newton, and has remained a source of prejudice against "action at a distance." In philosophy it has led to a denial of transient action, and thence to monism or Leibnizian monadism. Like the analogous maxim concerning temporal contiguity, it rests upon the assumption that causes "operate," i.e. that they are in some obscure way analogous to volitions. And, as in the case of temporal contiguity, the inferences drawn from this maxim are wholly groundless.

I return now to the question, What law or laws can be found to take the place of the supposed law of causality?

First, without passing beyond such uniformities of sequence as are contemplated by the traditional law, we may admit that, if any such sequence has been observed in a great many cases, and has never been found to fail, there is an inductive probability that it will be found to hold in future cases. If stones have hitherto been found to break windows, it is probable that they will continue to do so. This, of course, assumes the inductive principle, of which the truth may reasonably be questioned; but as this principle is not our present concern, I shall in this discussion treat it as indubitable. We may then say, in the case of any such frequently observed sequence, that the earlier event is the *cause* and the later event the *effect*.

Several considerations, however, make such special sequences very different from the traditional relation of cause and effect. In the first place, the sequence, in any hitherto unobserved instance, is no more than probable, whereas the relation of cause and effect was supposed to be necessary. I do not mean by this merely that we are not sure of having discovered a true case of cause and effect; I mean that, even when we have a case of cause and effect in our present sense, all that is meant is that on grounds of observation, it is probable that when one occurs the other will also occur. Thus in our present sense, A may be the cause of B even if there actually are cases where B does not follow A. Striking a match will be the cause of its igniting, in spite of the fact that some matches are damp and fail to ignite.

In the second place, it will not be assumed that *every* event has some antecedent which is its cause in this sense; we shall only believe in causal sequences where we find them, without any presumption that they always are to be found.

In the third place, *any* case of sufficiently frequent sequence will be causal in our present sense; for example, we shall not refuse to say that night is the cause of day. Our repugnance to saying this arises from the ease with which we can imagine the sequence to fail, but owing to the fact that cause and effect must be separated by a finite interval of time, *any* such sequence *might* fail through the interposition of other circumstances in the interval. Mill, discussing this instance of night and day, says:—

"It is necessary to our using the word cause, that we should believe not only that the antecedent always *has* been followed by the consequent, but that as long as the present constitution of things endures, it always *will* be so."[39]

In this sense, we shall have to give up the hope of finding causal laws such as Mill contemplated; any causal sequence which we have observed may at any moment be falsified without a falsification of any laws of the kind that the more advanced sciences aim at establishing.

In the fourth place, such laws of probable sequence, though useful in daily life and in the infancy of a science, tend to be displaced by quite different laws as soon as a science is successful. The law of gravitation will illustrate what occurs in any advanced science. In the motions of mutually gravitating bodies, there is nothing that can be called a cause, and nothing that can be called an effect; there is merely a formula. Certain differential equations can be found, which hold at every instant for every particle of the system, and which, given the configuration and velocities at one instant, or the configurations at two instants, render the configuration at any other earlier or later instant theoretically calculable. That is to say, the configuration at any instant is a function of that instant and the configurations at two given instants. This statement holds throughout physics, and not only in the special case of gravitation. But there is nothing that could be properly called "cause" and nothing that could be properly called "effect" in such a system.

No doubt the reason why the old "law of causality" has so long continued to pervade the books of philosophers is simply that the idea of a function is unfamiliar to most of them, and therefore they seek an unduly simplified statement. There is no question of repetitions of the "same" cause producing the "same" effect; it is not in any sameness of causes and effects that the constancy of scientific law consists, but in sameness of relations. And even "sameness of relations" is too simple a phrase; "sameness of differential equations" is the only correct phrase. It is impossible to state this accurately in non-mathematical language; the nearest approach would be as follows: "There is a constant relation between the state of the universe at any instant and the rate of change in the rate at which any part of the universe is changing at that instant, and this relation is many-one, i.e. such that the rate of change in the rate of change is determinate when the state of the universe is given." If the "law of causality" is to be something actually discoverable in the practice of science, the above proposition has a better right to the name than any "law of causality" to be found in the books of philosophers.

In regard to the above principle, several observations must be made—

(1) No one can pretend that the above principle is *a priori* or self-evident or a "necessity of thought." Nor is it, in any sense, a premiss of science: it is an empirical generalisation from a number of laws which are themselves empirical generalisations.

(2) The law makes no difference between past and future: the future "determines" the past in exactly the same sense in which the past "determines" the future. The word "determine,"

here, has a purely logical significance: a certain number of variables "determine" another variable if that other variable is a function of them.

(3) The law will not be empirically verifiable unless the course of events within some sufficiently small volume will be approximately the same in any two states of the universe which only differ in regard to what is at a considerable distance from the small volume in question. For example, motions of planets in the solar system must be approximately the same however the fixed stars may be distributed, provided that all the fixed stars are very much farther from the sun than the planets are. If gravitation varied directly as the distance, so that the most remote stars made the most difference to the motions of the planets, the world might be just as regular and just as much subject to mathematical laws as it is at present, but we could never discover the fact.

(4) Although the old "law of causality" is not assumed by science, something which we may call the "uniformity of nature" is assumed, or rather is accepted on inductive grounds. The uniformity of nature does not assert the trivial principle "same cause, same effect," but the principle of the permanence of laws. That is to say, when a law exhibiting, e.g. an acceleration as a function of the configuration has been found to hold throughout the observable past, it is expected that it will continue to hold in the future, or that, if it does not itself hold, there is some other law, agreeing with the supposed law as regards the past, which will hold for the future. The ground of this principle is simply the inductive ground that it has been found to be true in very many instances; hence the principle cannot be considered certain, but only probable to a degree which cannot be accurately estimated.

The uniformity of nature, in the above sense, although it is assumed in the practice of science, must not, in its generality, be regarded as a kind of major premiss, without which all scientific reasoning would be in error. The assumption that *all* laws of nature are permanent has, of course, less probability than the assumption that this or that particular law is permanent; and the assumption that a particular law is permanent for all time has less probability than the assumption that it will be valid up to such and such a date. Science, in any given case, will assume what the case requires, but no more. In constructing the *Nautical Almanac* for 1915 it will assume that the law of gravitation will remain true up to the end of that year; but it will make no assumption as to 1916 until it comes to the next volume of the almanac. This procedure is, of course, dictated by the fact that the uniformity of nature is not known *a priori*, but is an empirical generalisation, like "all men are mortal." In all such cases, it is better to argue immediately from the given particular instances to the new instance, than to argue by way of a major premiss; the conclusion is only probable in either case, but acquires a higher probability by the former method than by the latter.

In all science we have to distinguish two sorts of laws: first, those that are empirically verifiable but probably only approximate; secondly, those that are not verifiable, but may be exact. The law of gravitation, for example, in its applications to the solar system, is only empirically verifiable when it is assumed that matter outside the solar system may be ignored for such purposes; we believe this to be only approximately true, but we cannot empirically verify the law of universal gravitation which we believe to be exact. This point is very important in connection with what we may call "relatively isolated systems." These may be defined as follows:—

A system relatively isolated during a given period is one which, within some assignable margin of error, will behave in the same way throughout that period, however the rest of the universe may be constituted.

A system may be called "practically isolated" during a given period if, although there *might* be states of the rest of the universe which would produce more than the assigned margin of error, there is reason to believe that such states do not in fact occur.

Strictly speaking, we ought to specify the respect in which the system is relatively isolated. For example, the earth is relatively isolated as regards falling bodies, but not as regards tides; it is *practically* isolated as regards economic phenomena, although, if Jevons' sunspot theory of commercial crises had been true, it would not have been even practically isolated in this respect.

It will be observed that we cannot prove in advance that a system is isolated. This will be inferred from the observed fact that approximate uniformities can be stated for this system alone. If the complete laws for the whole universe were known, the isolation of a system could be deduced from them; assuming, for example, the law of universal gravitation, the practical isolation of the solar system in this respect can be deduced by the help of the fact that there is very little matter in its neighbourhood. But it should be observed that isolated systems are only important as providing a possibility of *discovering* scientific laws; they have no theoretical importance in the finished structure of a science.

The case where one event A is said to "cause" another event B, which philosophers take as fundamental, is really only the most simplified instance of a practically isolated system. It may happen that, as a result of general scientific laws, whenever A occurs throughout a certain period, it is followed by B; in that case, A and B form a system which is practically isolated throughout that period. It is, however, to be regarded as a piece of good fortune if this occurs; it will always be due to special circumstances, and would not have been true if the rest of the universe had been different though subject to the same laws.

The essential function which causality has been supposed to perform is the possibility of inferring the future from the past, or, more generally, events at any time from events at certain assigned times. Any system in which such inference is possible may be called a "deterministic" system. We may define a deterministic system as follows:—
<
div class="block">
A system is said to be "deterministic" when, given certain data, e_1, e_2, ... , e_n, at times t_1, t_2, ... , t_n respectively, concerning this system, if E_t is the state of the system at any time t, there is a functional relation of the form
<
div class="block">
$E_t = f(e_1, t_1, e_2, t_2, ... , e_n, t_n, t)$.   (A)

The system will be "deterministic throughout a given period" if t, in the above formula, may be any time within that period, though outside that period the formula may be no longer true. If the universe, as a whole, is such a system, determinism is true of the universe; if not, not. A system which is part of a deterministic system I shall call "determined"; one which is not part of any such system I shall call "capricious."

The events $e_1, e_2, \ldots, e_n$ I shall call "determinants" of the system. It is to be observed that a system which has one set of determinants will in general have many. In the case of the motions of the planets, for example, the configurations of the solar system at any two given times will be determinants.

We may take another illustration from the hypothesis of psycho-physical parallelism. Let us assume, for the purposes of this illustration, that to a given state of brain a given state of mind always corresponds, and vice versa, i.e. that there is a one-one relation between them, so that each is a function of the other. We may also assume, what is practically certain, that to a given state of a certain brain a given state of the whole material universe corresponds, since it is highly improbable that a given brain is ever twice in exactly the same state. Hence there will be a one-one relation between the state of a given person's mind and the state of the whole material universe. It follows that, if n states of the material universe are determinants of the material universe, then n states of a given man's mind are determinants of the whole material and mental universe—assuming, that is to say, that psycho-physical parallelism is true.

The above illustration is important in connection with a certain confusion which seems to have beset those who have philosophised on the relation of mind and matter. It is often thought that, if the state of the mind is determinate when the state of the brain is given, and if the material world forms a deterministic system, then mind is "subject" to matter in some sense in which matter is not "subject" to mind. But if the state of the brain is also determinate when the state of the mind is given, it must be exactly as true to regard matter as subject to mind as it would be to regard mind as subject to matter. We could, theoretically, work out the history of mind without ever mentioning matter, and then, at the end, deduce that matter must meanwhile have gone through the corresponding history. It is true that if the relation of brain to mind were many-one, not one-one, there would be a one-sided dependence of mind on brain, while conversely, if the relation were one-many, as Bergson supposes, there would be a one-aided dependence of brain on mind. But the dependence involved is, in any case, only logical; it does not mean that we shall be compelled to do things we desire not to do, which is what people instinctively imagine it to mean.

As another illustration we may take the case of mechanism and teleology. A system may be defined as "mechanical" when it has a set of determinants that are purely material, such as the positions of certain pieces of matter at certain times. It is an open question whether the world of mind and matter, as we know it, is a mechanical system or not; let us suppose, for the sake of argument, that it is a mechanical system. This supposition—so I contend—throws no light whatever on the question whether the universe is or is not a "teleological" system. It is difficult to define accurately what is meant by a "teleological" system, but the argument is not much affected by the particular definition we adopt. Broadly, a teleological system is one in which purposes are realised, i.e. in which certain desires—those that are deeper or nobler or more fundamental or more universal or what not—are followed by their realisation. Now the fact—if it be a fact—that the universe is mechanical has no bearing whatever on the question whether it is teleological in the above sense. There might be a mechanical system in which all wishes were realised, and there might be one in which all wishes were thwarted. The question whether, or how far, our actual world is teleological, cannot, therefore, be settled by proving that it is mechanical, and the desire that it should be teleological is no ground for wishing it to be not mechanical.

There is, in all these questions, a very great difficulty in avoiding confusion between what we can infer and what is in fact determined. Let us consider, for a moment, the various senses in which the future may be "determined." There is one sense—and a very important one—in which it is determined quite independently of scientific laws, namely, the sense that it will be what it will be. We all regard the past as determined simply by the fact that it has happened; but for the accident that memory works backward and not forward, we should regard the future as equally determined by the fact that it will happen. "But," we are told, "you cannot alter the past, while you can to some extent alter the future." This view seems to me to rest upon just those errors in regard to causation which it has been my object to remove. You cannot make the past other than it was—true, but this is a mere application of the law of contradiction. If you already know what the past was, obviously it is useless to wish it different. But also you cannot make the future other than it will be; this again is an application of the law of contradiction. And if you happen to know the future—e.g. in the case of a forthcoming eclipse—it is just as useless to wish it different as to wish the past different. "But," it will be rejoined, "our wishes can *cause* the future, sometimes, to be different from what it would be if they did not exist, and they can have no such effect upon the past." This, again, is a mere tautology. An effect being *defined* as something subsequent to its cause, obviously we can have no *effect* upon the past. But that does not mean that the past would not have been different if our present wishes had been different. Obviously, our present wishes are conditioned by the past, and therefore could not have been different unless the past had been different; therefore, if our present wishes were different, the past would be different. Of course, the past cannot be different from what it was, but no more can our present wishes be different from what they are; this again is merely the law of contradiction. The facts seem to be merely (1) that wishing generally depends upon ignorance, and is therefore commoner in regard to the future than in regard to the past; (2) that where a wish concerns the future, it and its realisation very often form a "practically independent system," i.e. many wishes regarding the future are realised. But there seems no doubt that the main difference in our feelings arises from the accidental fact that the past but not the future can be known by memory.

Although the sense of "determined" in which the future is determined by the mere fact that it will be what it will be is sufficient (at least so it seems to me) to refute some opponents of determinism, notably M. Bergson and the pragmatists, yet it is not what most people have in mind when they speak of the future as determined. What they have in mind is a formula by means of which the future can be exhibited, and at least theoretically calculated, as a function of the past. But at this point we meet with a great difficulty, which besets what has been said above about deterministic systems, as well as what is said by others.

If formulæ of any degree of complexity, however great, are admitted, it would seem that any system, whose state at a given moment is a function of certain measurable quantities, must be a deterministic system. Let us consider, in illustration, a single material particle, whose co-ordinates at time t are x_t, y_t, z_t. Then, however, the particle moves, there must be, theoretically, functions f_1, f_2, f_3, such that
<
div class="block">
$$x_t = f_1(t), \qquad y_t = f_2(t), \qquad z_t = f_3(t).$$
It follows that, theoretically, the whole state of the material universe at time t must be capable of being exhibited as a function of t. Hence our universe will be deterministic in the sense defined above. But if this be true, no information is conveyed about the universe in stating that it is deterministic. It is true that the formulæ involved may be of strictly infinite complexity, and therefore not practically capable of being written down or apprehended. But except from the point of view of our knowledge, this might seem to be a detail: in itself, if the above considerations are sound, the material universe *must* be deterministic, *must* be subject to laws.

This, however, is plainly not what was intended. The difference between this view and the view intended may be seen as follows. Given some formula which fits the facts hitherto—say the law of gravitation—there will be an infinite number of other formulæ, not empirically distinguishable from it in the past, but diverging from it more and more in the future. Hence, even assuming that there are persistent laws, we shall have no reason for assuming that the law of the inverse square will hold in future; it may be some other hitherto indistinguishable law that will hold. We cannot say that *every* law which has held hitherto must hold in the future, because past facts which obey one law will also obey others, hitherto indistinguishable but diverging in future. Hence there must, at every moment, be laws hitherto unbroken which are now broken for the first time. What science does, in fact, is to select the *simplest* formula that will fit the facts. But this, quite obviously, is merely a methodological precept, not a law of Nature. If the simplest formula ceases, after a time, to be applicable, the simplest formula that remains applicable is selected, and science has no sense that an axiom has been falsified. We are thus left with the brute fact that, in many departments of science, quite simple laws have hitherto been found to hold. This fact cannot be regarded as having any *a priori* ground, nor can it be used to support inductively the opinion that the same laws will continue; for at every moment laws hitherto true are being falsified, though in the advanced sciences these laws are less simple than those that have remained true. Moreover it would be fallacious to argue inductively from the state of the advanced sciences to the future state of the others, for it may well be that the advanced sciences are advanced simply because, hitherto, their subject-matter has obeyed simple and easily ascertainable laws, while the subject-matter of other sciences has not done so.

The difficulty we have been considering seems to be met partly, if not wholly, by the principle that the *time* must not enter explicitly into our formulæ. All mechanical laws exhibit acceleration as a function of configuration, not of configuration and time jointly; and this principle of the irrelevance of the time may be extended to all scientific laws. In fact we might interpret the "uniformity of nature" as meaning just this, that no scientific law involves the time as an argument, unless, of course, it is given in an integrated form, in which case *lapse* of time, though not absolute time, may appear in our formulæ. Whether this consideration suffices to overcome our difficulty completely, I do not know; but in any case it does much to diminish it.

It will serve to illustrate what has been said if we apply it to the question of free will.

(1) Determinism in regard to the will is the doctrine that our volitions belong to some deterministic system, i.e. are "determined" in the sense defined above. Whether this doctrine is true or false, is a mere question of fact; no *a priori* considerations (if our previous discussions have been correct) can exist on either side. On the one hand, there is no *a priori* category of causality, but merely certain observed uniformities. As a matter of fact, there are observed uniformities in regard to

volitions; thus there is some empirical evidence that volitions are determined. But it would be very rash to maintain that the evidence is overwhelming, and it is quite possible that some volitions, as well as some other things, are not determined, except in the sense in which we found that everything must be determined.

(2) But, on the other hand, the subjective sense of freedom, sometimes alleged against determinism, has no bearing on the question whatever. The view that it has a bearing rests upon the belief that causes compel their effects, or that nature enforces obedience to its laws as governments do. These are mere anthropomorphic superstitions, due to assimilation of causes with volitions and of natural laws with human edicts. We feel that our will is not compelled, but that only means that it is not other than we choose it to be. It is one of the demerits of the traditional theory of causality that it has created an artificial opposition between determinism and the freedom of which we are introspectively conscious.

(3) Besides the general question whether volitions are determined, there is the further question whether they are *mechanically* determined, i.e. whether they are part of what was above defined as a mechanical system. This is the question whether they form part of a system with purely material determinants, i.e. whether there are laws which, given certain material data, make all volitions functions of those data. Here again, there is empirical evidence up to a point, but it is not conclusive in regard to all volitions. It is important to observe, however that even if volitions are part of a mechanical system, this by no means implies any supremacy of matter over mind. It may well be that the same system which is susceptible of material determinants is also susceptible of mental determinants; thus a mechanical system may be determined by sets of volitions, as well as by sets of material facts. It would seem, therefore, that the reasons which make people dislike the view that volitions are mechanically determined are fallacious.

(4) The notion of *necessity*, which is often associated with determinism, is a confused notion not legitimately deducible from determinism. Three meanings are commonly confounded when necessity is spoken of:—

(α) An *action* is necessary when it will be performed however much the agent may wish to do otherwise. Determinism does not imply that actions are necessary in this sense.

(β) A *propositional function* is necessary when all its values are true. This sense is not relevant to our present discussion.

(γ) A *proposition* is necessary with respect to a given constituent when it is the value, with that constituent as argument, of a necessary propositional function, in other words, when it remains true however that constituent may be varied. In this sense, in a deterministic system, the connection of a volition with its determinants is necessary, if the time at which the determinants occur be taken as the constituent to be varied, the time-interval between the determinants and the volition being kept constant. But this sense of necessity is purely logical, and has no emotional importance.

We may now sum up our discussion of causality. We found first that the law of causality, as usually stated by philosophers, is false, and is not employed in science. We then considered the nature of scientific laws, and found that, instead of stating that one event A is always followed by another event B, they stated functional relations between certain events at certain times, which we called determinants, and other events at earlier or later times or at the same time. We were unable to find any *a priori* category involved: the existence of scientific laws appeared as a purely empirical fact, not necessarily universal, except in a trivial and scientifically useless form. We found that a system with one set of determinants may very likely have other sets of a quite different kind, that, for example, a mechanically determined system may also be teleologically or volitionally determined. Finally we considered the problem of free will: here we found that the reasons for supposing volitions to be determined are strong but not conclusive, and we decided that even if volitions are mechanically determined, that is no reason for denying freedom in the sense revealed by introspection, or for supposing that mechanical events are not determined by volitions. The problem of free will *versus* determinism is therefore, if we were right, mainly illusory, but in part not yet capable of being decisively solved.

Footnotes

[35] A propositional function is an expression containing a variable, or undetermined constituent, and becoming a proposition as soon as a definite value is assigned to the variable. Examples are: "A is A," "x is a number." The variable is called the *argument* of the function.
    [36] *Logic*, Bk. III, Chap. V, § 2.
    [37] *Time and Free Will*, p. 199.
    [38] *Time and Free Will.* p. 202.
    [39] *Loc. cit.*, § 6
<
   div class="footnote">
17 18 19

10

Knowledge by Acquaintance and Knowledge by Description

The object of the following paper is to consider what it is that we know in cases where we know propositions about "the so-and-so" without knowing who or what the so-and-so is. For example, I know that the candidate who gets most votes will be elected, though I do not know who is the candidate who will get most votes. The problem I wish to consider is: What do we know in these cases, where the subject is merely described? I have considered this problem elsewhere[40] from a purely logical point of view; but in what follows I wish to consider the question in relation to theory of knowledge as well as in relation to logic, and in view of the above-mentioned logical discussions, I shall in this paper make the logical portion as brief as possible.

In order to make clear the antithesis between "acquaintance" and "description," I shall first of all try to explain what I mean by "acquaintance." I say that I am *acquainted* with an object when I have a direct cognitive relation to that object, i.e. when I am directly aware of the object itself. When I speak of a cognitive relation here, I do not mean the sort of relation which constitutes judgment, but the sort which constitutes presentation. In fact, I think the relation of subject and object which I call acquaintance is simply the converse of the relation of object and subject which constitutes presentation. That is, to say that S has acquaintance with O is essentially the same thing as to say that O is presented to S. But the associations and natural extensions of the word *acquaintance* are different from those of the word *presentation*. To begin with, as in most cognitive words, it is natural to say that I am acquainted with an object even at moments when it is not actually before my mind, provided it has been before my mind, and will be again whenever occasion arises. This is the same sense in which I am said to know that 2+2=4 even when I am thinking of something else. In the second place, the word *acquaintance* is designed to emphasise, more than the word *presentation*, the relational character of the fact with which we are concerned. There is, to my mind, a danger that, in speaking of presentation, we may so emphasis the object as to lose sight of the subject. The result of this is either to lead to the view that there is no subject, whence we arrive at materialism; or to lead to the view that what is presented is part of the subject, whence we arrive at idealism, and should arrive at solipsism but for the most desperate contortions. Now I wish to preserve the dualism of subject and object in my terminology, because this dualism seems to me a fundamental fact concerning cognition. Hence I prefer the word *acquaintance* because it emphasises the need of a subject which is acquainted.

When we ask what are the kinds of objects with which we are acquainted, the first and most obvious example is *sense-data*. When I see a colour or hear a noise, I have direct acquaintance with the colour or the noise. The sense-datum with which I am acquainted in these cases is generally, if not always, complex. This is particularly obvious in the case of sight. I do not mean, of course, merely that the supposed physical object is complex, but that the direct sensible object is complex and contains parts with spatial relations. Whether it is possible to be aware of a complex without being aware of its constituents is not an easy question, but on the whole it would seem that there is no reason why it should not be possible. This question arises in an acute form in connection with self-consciousness, which we must now briefly consider.

In introspection, we seem to be immediately aware of varying complexes, consisting of objects in various cognitive and conative relations to ourselves. When I see the sun, it often happens that I am aware of my seeing the sun, in addition to being aware of the sun; and when I desire food, it often happens that I am aware of my desire for food. But it is hard to discover any state of mind in which I am aware of myself alone, as opposed to a complex of which I am a constituent. The question of the nature of self-consciousness is too large and too slightly connected with our subject, to be argued at length here. It is difficult, but probably not impossible, to account for plain facts if we assume that we do not have acquaintance with ourselves. It is plain that we are not only *acquainted* with the complex "Self-acquainted-with-A," but we also *know* the proposition "I am acquainted with A." Now here the complex has been analysed, and if "I" does not stand for something which is a direct object of acquaintance, we shall have to suppose that "I" is something known by description. If we wished to maintain the view that there is no acquaintance with Self, we might argue as follows: We are acquainted with *acquaintance*, and we know that it is a relation. Also we are acquainted with a complex in which we perceive that acquaintance is the relating relation. Hence we know that this complex must have a constituent which is that which is acquainted, i.e. must have a subject-term as well as an object-term. This subject-term we define as "I." Thus "I" means "the subject-term in awarenesses of which *I* am aware." But as a definition this cannot be regarded as a happy effort. It would seem necessary, therefore, either to suppose that I am acquainted with myself, and that "I," therefore, requires no definition, being merely the proper name of a certain object, or to find some other analysis of self-consciousness. Thus self-consciousness cannot be regarded as throwing light on the question whether we can know a complex without knowing its constituents. This question, however, is not important for our present purposes, and I shall therefore not discuss it further.

The awarenesses we have considered so far have all been awarenesses of particular existents, and might all in a large sense be called sense-data. For, from the point of view of theory of knowledge, introspective knowledge is exactly on a level with knowledge derived from sight or hearing. But, in addition to awareness of the above kind of objects, which may be called awareness of *particulars*; we have also (though not quite in the same sense) what may be called awareness of *universals*. Awareness of universals is called *conceiving*, and a universal of which we are aware is called a *concept*. Not only are we aware of particular yellows, but if we have seen a sufficient number of yellows and have sufficient intelligence, we are aware of the universal *yellow*; this universal is the subject in such judgments as "yellow differs from blue" or "yellow resembles blue less than green does." And the universal yellow is the predicate in such judgments as "this is yellow," where "this" is a particular sense-datum. And universal relations, too, are objects of awarenesses; up and down, before and after, resemblance, desire, awareness itself, and so on, would seem to be all of them objects of which we can be aware.

In regard to relations, it might be urged that we are never aware of the universal relation itself, but only of complexes in which it is a constituent. For example, it may be said that we do not know directly such a relation as *before*, though we understand such a proposition as "this is before that," and may be directly aware of such a complex as "this being before that." This view, however, is difficult to reconcile with the fact that we often know propositions in which the relation is the subject, or in which the relata are not definite given objects, but "anything." For example, we know that if one thing is before another, and the other before a third, then the first is before the third; and here the things concerned are not definite things, but "anything." It is hard to see how we could know such a fact about "before" unless we were acquainted with "before," and not merely with actual particular cases of one given object being before another given object. And more directly: A judgment such as "this is before that," where this judgment is derived from awareness of a complex, constitutes an analysis, and we should not understand the analysis if we were not acquainted with the meaning of the terms employed. Thus we must suppose that we are acquainted with the meaning of "before," and not merely with instances of it.

There are thus at least two sorts of objects of which we are aware, namely, particulars and universals. Among particulars I include all existents, and all complexes of which one or more constituents are existents, such as this-before-that, this-above-that, the-yellowness-of-this. Among universals I include all objects of which no particular is a constituent. Thus the disjunction "universal-particular" includes all objects. We might also call it the disjunction "abstract-concrete." It is not quite parallel with the opposition "concept-percept," because things remembered or imagined belong with particulars, but can hardly be called percepts. (On the other hand, universals with which we are acquainted may be identified with concepts.)

It will be seen that among the objects with which we are acquainted are not included physical objects (as opposed to sense-data), nor other people's minds. These things are known to us by what I call "knowledge by description," which we must now consider.

By a "description" I mean any phrase of the form "a so-and-so" or "the so-and-so." A phrase of the form "a so-and-so" I shall call an "ambiguous" description; a phrase of the form "the so-and-so" (in the singular) I shall call a "definite" description. Thus "a man" is an ambiguous description, and "the man with the iron mask" is a definite description. There are various problems connected with ambiguous descriptions, but I pass them by, since they do not directly concern the matter I wish to discuss. What I wish to discuss is the nature of our knowledge concerning objects in cases where we know that there is an object answering to a definite description, though we are not *acquainted* with any such object. This is a matter which is concerned exclusively with *definite* descriptions. I shall, therefore, in the sequel, speak simply of "descriptions" when I mean "definite descriptions." Thus a description will mean any phrase of the form "the so-and-so" in the singular.

I shall say that an object is "known by description" when we know that it is "*the* so-and-so," i.e. when we know that there is one object, and no more, having a certain property; and it will generally be implied that we do not have knowledge of the same object by acquaintance. We know that the man with the iron mask existed, and many propositions are known about him; but we do not know who he was. We know that the candidate who gets most votes will be elected, and in this case we are very likely also acquainted (in the only sense in which one can be acquainted with some one else) with the man who is, in fact, the candidate who will get most votes, but we do not know which of the candidates he is, i.e. we do not know any proposition of the form "A is the candidate who will get most votes" where A is one of the candidates by name. We shall say that we have "*merely* descriptive knowledge" of the so-and-so when, although we know that the so-and-so exists, and although we may possibly be acquainted with the object which is, in fact, the so-and-so, yet we do not know any proposition "*a* is the so-and-so," where *a* is something with which we are acquainted.

When we say "the so-and-so exists," we mean that there is just one object which is the so-and-so. The proposition "*a* is the so-and-so" means that *a* has the property so-and-so, and nothing else has. "Sir Joseph Larmor is the Unionist candidate" means "Sir Joseph Larmor is a Unionist candidate, and no one else is." "The Unionist candidate exists" means "some one is a Unionist candidate, and no one else is." Thus, when we are acquainted with an object which we know to be the so-and-so, we know that the so-and-so exists but we may know that the so-and-so exists when we are not acquainted with any object which we know to be the so-and-so, and even when we are not acquainted with any object which, in fact, is the so-and-so.

Common words, even proper names, are usually really descriptions. That is to say, the thought in the mind of a person using a proper name correctly can generally only be expressed explicitly if we replace the proper name by a description. Moreover, the description required to express the thought will vary for different people, or for the same person at different times. The only thing constant (so long as the name is rightly used) is the object to which the name applies. But so long as this remains constant, the particular description involved usually makes no difference to the truth or falsehood of the proposition in which the name appears.

Let us take some illustrations. Suppose some statement made about Bismarck. Assuming that there is such a thing as direct acquaintance with oneself, Bismarck himself might have used his name directly to designate the particular person with whom he was acquainted. In this case, if he made a judgment about himself, he himself might be a constituent of the judgment. Here the proper name has the direct use which it always wishes to have, as simply standing for a certain object, and not for a description of the object. But if a person who knew Bismarck made a judgment about him, the case is different. What this person was acquainted with were certain sense-data which he connected (rightly, we will suppose) with Bismarck's body. His body as a physical object, and still more his mind, were only known as the body and the mind connected with these sense-data. That is, they were known by description. It is, of course, very much a matter of chance which characteristics of a man's appearance will come into a friend's mind when he thinks of him; thus the description actually in the friend's mind is accidental. The essential point is that he knows that the various descriptions all apply to the same entity, in spite of not being acquainted with the entity in question.

When we, who did not know Bismarck, make a judgment about him, the description in our minds will probably be some more or less vague mass of historical knowledge—far more, in most cases, than is required to identify him. But, for the sake of illustration, let us assume that we think of him as "the first Chancellor of the German Empire." Here all the words are abstract except "German." The word "German" will again have different meanings for different people. To some it will recall travels in Germany, to some the look of Germany on the map, and so on. But if we are to obtain a description which we know to be applicable, we shall be compelled, at some point, to bring in a reference to a particular with which we are acquainted. Such reference is involved in any mention of past, present, and future (as opposed to definite dates), or of here and there, or of what others have told us. Thus it would seem that, in some way or other, a description known to be applicable to a particular must involve some reference to a particular with which we are acquainted, if our knowledge about the thing described is not to be merely what follows logically from the description. For example, "the most long-lived of men" is a description which must apply to some man, but we can make no judgments concerning this man which involve knowledge about him beyond what the description gives. If, however, we say, "the first Chancellor of the German Empire was an astute diplomatist," we can only be assured of the truth of our judgment in virtue of something with which we are acquainted—usually a testimony heard or read. Considered psychologically, apart from the information we convey to others, apart from the fact about the actual Bismarck, which gives importance to our judgment, the thought we really have contains the one or more particulars involved, and otherwise consists wholly of concepts. All names of places—London, England, Europe, the earth, the Solar System—similarly involve, when used, descriptions which start from some one or more particulars with which we are acquainted. I suspect that even the Universe, as considered by metaphysics, involves such a connection with particulars. In logic, on the contrary, where we are concerned not merely with what does exist, but with whatever might or could exist or be, no reference to actual particulars is involved.

It would seem that, when we make a statement about something only known by description, we often *intend* to make our statement, not in the form involving the description, but about the actual thing described. That is to say, when we say anything about Bismarck, we should like, if we could, to make the judgment which Bismarck alone can make, namely, the judgment of which he himself is a constituent. In this we are necessarily defeated, since the actual Bismarck is unknown to us. But we know that there is an object B called Bismarck, and that B was an astute diplomatist. We can thus *describe* the proposition we should like to affirm, namely, "B was an astute diplomatist," where B is the object which was Bismarck. What enables us to communicate in spite of the varying descriptions we employ is that we know there is a true proposition concerning the actual Bismarck, and that, however we may vary the description (so long as the description is correct), the proposition described is still the same. This proposition, which is described and is known to be true, is what interests us; but we are not acquainted with the proposition itself, and do not know *it*, though we know it is true.

It will be seen that there are various stages in the removal from acquaintance with particulars: there is Bismarck to people who knew him, Bismarck to those who only know of him through history, the man with the iron mask, the longest-lived of men. These are progressively further removed from acquaintance with particulars, and there is a similar hierarchy in the region of universals. Many universals, like many particulars, are only known to us by description. But here, as in the case of particulars, knowledge concerning what is known by description is ultimately reducible to knowledge concerning what is known by acquaintance.

The fundamental epistemological principle in the analysis of propositions containing descriptions is this: *Every proposition which we can understand must be composed wholly of constituents with which we are acquainted.* From what has been said already, it will be plain why I advocate this principle, and how I propose to meet the case of propositions which at first sight contravene it. Let us begin with the reasons for supposing the principle true.

The chief reason for supposing the principle true is that it seems scarcely possible to believe that we can make a judgment or entertain a supposition without knowing what it is that we are judging or supposing about. If we make a judgment about (say) Julius Cæsar, it is plain that the actual person who was Julius Cæsar is not a constituent of the judgment. But before going further, it may be well to explain what I mean when I say that this or that is a constituent of a judgment, or of a proposition which we understand. To begin with judgments: a judgment, as an occurrence, I take to be a relation of a mind to several entities, namely, the entities which compose what is judged. If, e.g. I judge that A loves B, the judgment as an event consists in the existence, at a certain moment, of a specific four-term relation, called *judging*, between me and A and love and B. That is to say, at the time when I judge, there is a certain complex whose terms are myself and A and love and B, and whose relating relation is *judging*. My reasons for this view have been set forth elsewhere,[41] and I shall not repeat them here. Assuming this view of judgment, the constituents of the judgment are simply the constituents of the complex which is the judgment. Thus, in the above case, the constituents are myself and A and love and B and judging. But myself and judging are constituents shared by all my judgments; thus the *distinctive* constituents of the particular judgment in question are A and love and B. Coming now to what is meant by "understanding a proposition," I should say that there is another relation possible between me and A and love and B, which is called my *supposing* that A loves B.[42] When we can *suppose* that A loves B, we "understand the proposition" *A loves B*. Thus we often understand a proposition in cases where we have not enough knowledge to make a judgment. Supposing, like judging, is a many-term relation, of which a mind is one term. The other terms of the relation are called the constituents of the proposition supposed. Thus the principle which I enunciated may be re-stated as follows: *Whenever a relation of supposing or judging occurs, the terms to which the supposing or judging mind is related by the relation of supposing or judging must be terms with which the mind in question is acquainted.* This is merely to say that we cannot make a judgment or a supposition without knowing what it is that we are making our judgment or supposition about. It seems to me that the truth of this principle is evident as soon as the principle is understood; I shall, therefore, in what follows, assume the principle, and use it as a guide in analysing judgments that contain descriptions.

Returning now to Julius Cæsar, I assume that it will be admitted that he himself is not a constituent of any judgment which I can make. But at this point it is necessary to examine the view that judgments are composed of something called "ideas," and that it is the "idea" of Julius Cæsar that is a constituent of my judgment. I believe the plausibility of this view rests upon a failure to form a right theory of descriptions. We may mean by my "idea" of Julius Cæsar the things that I know about him, e.g. that he conquered Gaul, was assassinated on the Ides of March, and is a plague to schoolboys. Now I am admitting, and indeed contending, that in order to discover what is actually in my mind when I judge about Julius Cæsar, we must substitute for the proper name a description made up of some of the things I know about him. (A description which will often serve to express my thought is "the man whose name was *Julius Cæsar.*" For whatever else I may have forgotten about him, it is plain that when I mention him I have not forgotten that that was his name.) But although I think the theory that judgments consist of ideas may have been suggested in some such way, yet I think the theory itself is fundamentally mistaken. The view seems to be that there is some mental existent which may be called the "idea" of something outside the mind of the person who has the idea, and that, since judgment is a mental event, its constituents must be constituents of the mind of the person judging. But in this view ideas become a veil between us and outside things—we never really, in knowledge, attain to the things we are supposed to be knowing about, but only to the ideas of those things. The relation of mind, idea, and object, on this view, is utterly obscure, and, so far as I can see, nothing discoverable by inspection warrants the intrusion of the idea between the mind and the object. I suspect that the view is fostered by the dislike of relations, and that it is felt the mind could not know objects unless there were something "in" the mind which could be called the state of knowing the object. Such a view, however, leads at once to a vicious endless regress, since the relation of idea to object will have to be explained by supposing that the idea itself has an idea of the object, and so on *ad infinitum*. I therefore see no reason to believe that, when we are acquainted with an object, there is in us something which can be called the "idea" of the object. On the contrary, I hold that acquaintance is wholly a relation, not demanding any such constituent of the mind as is supposed by advocates of "ideas." This is, of course, a large question, and one which would take us far from our subject if it were adequately discussed. I therefore content myself with the above indications, and with the corollary that, in judging, the actual objects concerning which we judge, rather than any supposed purely mental entities, are constituents of the complex which is the judgment.

When, therefore, I say that we must substitute for "Julius Cæsar" some description of Julius Cæsar, in order to discover the meaning of a judgment nominally about him, I am not saying that we must substitute an idea. Suppose our description is "the man whose name was *Julius Cæsar.*" Let our judgment be "Julius Cæsar was assassinated." Then it becomes "the man whose name was *Julius Cæsar* was assassinated." Here *Julius Cæsar* is a noise or shape with which we are acquainted, and all the other constituents of the judgment (neglecting the tense in "was") are *concepts* with which we are acquainted. Thus our judgment is wholly reduced to constituents with which we are acquainted, but Julius Cæsar himself has ceased to be a constituent of our judgment. This, however, requires a proviso, to be further explained shortly, namely that "the man whose name was *Julius Cæsar*" must not, as a whole, be a constituent of our judgment, that is to say, this phrase must not, as a whole, have a meaning which enters into the judgment. Any right analysis of the judgment, therefore, must break up this phrase, and not treat it as a subordinate complex which is part of the judgment. The judgment "the man whose name was *Julius Cæsar* was assassinated" may be interpreted as meaning "one and only one man was called *Julius Cæsar*, and that one was assassinated." Here it is plain that there is no constituent corresponding to the phrase "the man whose name was *Julius Cæsar*." Thus there is no reason to regard this phrase as expressing a constituent of the judgment, and we have seen that this phrase must be broken up if we are to be acquainted with all the constituents of the judgment. This conclusion, which we have reached from considerations concerned with the theory of knowledge, is also forced upon us by logical considerations, which must now be briefly reviewed.

It is common to distinguish two aspects, *meaning* and *denotation*, such phrases as "the author of Waverley." The meaning will be a certain complex, consisting (at least) of authorship and Waverley with some relation; the denotation will be Scott. Similarly "featherless bipeds" will have a complex meaning, containing as constituents the presence of two feet and the absence of feathers, while its denotation will be the class of men. Thus when we say "Scott is the author of Waverley" or "men are the same as featherless bipeds," we are asserting an identity of denotation, and this assertion is worth making because of the diversity of meaning.[43] I believe that the duality of meaning and denotation, though capable of a true interpretation, is misleading if taken as fundamental. The denotation, I believe, is not a constituent of the proposition, except in the case of proper names, i.e. of words which do not assign a property to an object, but merely and solely name it. And I should hold further that, in this sense, there are only two words which are strictly proper names of particulars, namely, "I" and "this."[44]

One reason for not believing the denotation to be a constituent of the proposition is that we may know the proposition even when we are not acquainted with the denotation. The proposition "the author of Waverley is a novelist" was known to people who did not know that "the author of Waverley" denoted Scott. This reason has been already sufficiently emphasised.

A second reason is that propositions concerning "the so-and-so" are possible even when "the so-and-so" has no denotation. Take, e.g. "the golden mountain does not exist" or "the round square is self-contradictory." If we are to preserve the duality of meaning and denotation, we have to say, with Meinong, that there are such objects as the golden mountain and the round square, although these objects do not have being. We even have to admit that the existent round square is existent, but does not exist.[45] Meinong does not regard this as a contradiction, but I fail to see that it is not one. Indeed, it seems to me evident that the judgment "there is no such object as the round square" does not presuppose that there is such an object. If this is admitted, however, we are led to the conclusion that, by parity of form, no judgment concerning "the so-and-so" actually involves the so-and-so as a constituent.

Miss Jones[46] contends that there is no difficulty in admitting contradictory predicates concerning such an object as "the present King of France," on the ground that this object is in itself contradictory. Now it might, of course, be argued that this object, unlike the round square, is not self-contradictory, but merely non-existent. This, however, would not go to the root of the matter. The real objection to such an argument is that the law of contradiction ought not to be stated in the traditional form "A is not both B and not B," but in the form "no proposition is both true and false." The traditional form only applies to certain propositions, namely, to those which attribute a predicate to a subject. When the law is stated of propositions, instead of being stated concerning subjects and predicates, it is at once evident that propositions about the present King of France or the round square can form no exception, but are just as incapable of being both true and false as other propositions. Miss Jones[47] argues that "Scott is the author of Waverley" asserts identity of denotation between *Scott* and *the author of Waverley*. But there is some difficulty in choosing among alternative meanings of this contention. In the first place, it should be observed that *the author of Waverley* is not a *mere* name, like *Scott*. *Scott* is merely a noise or shape conventionally used to designate a certain person; it gives us no information about that person, and has nothing that can be called meaning as opposed to denotation. (I neglect the fact, considered above, that even proper names, as a rule, really stand for descriptions.) But *the author of Waverley* is not merely conventionally a name for Scott; the element of mere convention belongs here to the separate words, *the* and *author* and *of* and

Waverley. Given what these words stand for, *the author of Waverley* is no longer arbitrary. When it is said that Scott is the author of Waverley, we are not stating that these are two *names* for one man, as we should be if we said "Scott is Sir Walter." A man's name is what he is called, but however much Scott had been called the author of Waverley, that would not have made him be the author; it was necessary for him actually to write Waverley, which was a fact having nothing to do with names.

If, then, we are asserting identity of denotation, we must not mean by *denotation* the mere relation of a name to the thing named. In fact, it would be nearer to the truth to say that the *meaning* of "Scott" is the *denotation* of "the author of Waverley." The relation of "Scott" to Scott is that "Scott" means Scott, just as the relation of "author" to the concept which is so called is that "author" means this concept. Thus if we distinguish meaning and denotation in "the author of Waverley," we shall have to say that "Scott" has meaning but not denotation. Also when we say "Scott is the author of Waverley," the *meaning* of "the author of Waverley" is relevant to our assertion. For if the denotation alone were relevant, any other phrase with the same denotation would give the same proposition. Thus "Scott is the author of Marmion" would be the same proposition as "Scott is the author of Waverley." But this is plainly not the case, since from the first we learn that Scott wrote Marmion and from the second we learn that he wrote Waverley, but the first tells us nothing about Waverley and the second nothing about Marmion. Hence the meaning of "the author of Waverley," as opposed to the denotation, is certainly relevant to "Scott is the author of Waverley."

We have thus agreed that "the author of Waverley" is not a mere name, and that its meaning is relevant in propositions in which it occurs. Thus if we are to say, as Miss Jones does, that "Scott is the author of Waverley" asserts an identity of denotation, we must regard the denotation of "the author of Waverley" as the denotation of what is *meant* by "the author of Waverley." Let us call the meaning of "the author of Waverley" M. Thus M is what "the author of Waverley" means. Then we are to suppose that "Scott is the author of Waverley" means "Scott is the denotation of M." But here we are explaining our proposition by another of the same form, and thus we have made no progress towards a real explanation. "The denotation of M," like "the author of Waverley," has both meaning and denotation, on the theory we are examining. If we call its meaning M', our proposition becomes "Scott is the denotation of M'." But this leads at once to an endless regress. Thus the attempt to regard our proposition as asserting identity of denotation breaks down, and it becomes imperative to find some other analysis. When this analysis has been completed, we shall be able to reinterpret the phrase "identity of denotation," which remains obscure so long as it is taken as fundamental.

The first point to observe is that, in any proposition about "the author of Waverley," provided Scott is not explicitly mentioned, the denotation itself, i.e. Scott, does not occur, but only the concept of denotation, which will be represented by a variable. Suppose we say "the author of Waverley was the author of Marmion," we are certainly not saying that both were Scott—we may have forgotten that there was such a person as Scott. We are saying that there is some man who was the author of Waverley and the author of Marmion. That is to say, there is some one who wrote Waverley and Marmion, and no one else wrote them. Thus the identity is that of a variable, i.e. of an indefinite subject, "some one." This is why we can understand propositions about "the author of Waverley," without knowing who he was. When we say "the author of Waverley was a poet," we mean "one and only one man wrote Waverley, and he was a poet"; when we say "the author of Waverley was Scott" we mean "one and only one man wrote Waverley, and he was Scott." Here the identity is between a variable, i.e. an indeterminate subject ("he"), and Scott; "the author of Waverley" has been analysed away, and no longer appears as a constituent of the proposition.[49]

The reason why it is imperative to analyse away the phrase "the author of Waverley" may be stated as follows. It is plain that when we say "the author of Waverley is the author of Marmion," the *is* expresses identity. We have seen also that the common *denotation*, namely Scott, is not a constituent of this proposition, while the *meanings* (if any) of "the author of Waverley" and "the author of Marmion" are not identical. We have seen also that, in any sense in which the meaning of a word is a constituent of a proposition in whose verbal expression the word occurs, "Scott" means the actual man Scott, in the same sense (so far as concerns our present discussion) in which "author" means a certain universal. Thus, if "the author of Waverley" were a subordinate complex in the above proposition, its *meaning* would have to be what was said to be identical with the *meaning* of "the author of Marmion." This is plainly not the case; and the only escape is to say that "the author of Waverley" does not, by itself, have a meaning, though phrases of which it is part do have a meaning. That is, in a right analysis of the above proposition, "the author of Waverley" must disappear. This is effected when the above proposition is analysed as meaning: "Some one wrote Waverley and no one else did, and that some one also wrote Marmion and no one else did." This may be more simply expressed by saying that the propositional function "x wrote Waverley and Marmion, and no one else did" is capable of truth, i.e. some value of x makes it true, but no other value does. Thus the true subject of our judgment is a propositional function, i.e. a complex containing an undetermined constituent, and becoming a proposition as soon as this constituent is determined.

We may now define the denotation of a phrase. If we know that the proposition "a is the so-and-so" is true, i.e. that a is so-and-so and nothing else is, we call a the denotation of the phrase "the so-and-so." A very great many of the propositions we naturally make about "the so-and-so" will remain true or remain false if we substitute a for "the so-and-so," where a is the denotation of "the so-and-so." Such propositions will also remain true or remain false if we substitute for "the so-and-so" any other phrase having the same denotation. Hence, as practical men, we become interested in the denotation more than in the description, since the denotation decides as to the truth or falsehood of so many statements in which the description occurs. Moreover, as we saw earlier in considering the relations of description and acquaintance, we often wish to reach the denotation, and are only hindered by lack of acquaintance: in such cases the description is merely the means we employ to get as near as possible to the denotation. Hence it naturally comes to be supposed that the denotation is part of the proposition in which the description occurs. But we have seen, both on logical and on epistemological grounds, that this is an error. The actual object (if any) which is the denotation is not (unless it is explicitly mentioned) a constituent of propositions in which descriptions occur; and this is the reason why, in order to understand such propositions, we need acquaintance with the constituents of the description, but do not need acquaintance with its denotation. The first result of analysis, when applied to propositions whose grammatical subject is "the so-and-so," is to substitute a variable as subject; i.e. we obtain a proposition of the form: "There is *something* which alone is so-and-so, and that *something* is such-and-such." The further analysis of propositions concerning "the so-and-so" is thus merged in the problem of the nature of the variable, i.e. of the meanings of *some*, *any*, and *all*. This is a difficult problem, concerning which I do not intend to say anything at present.

To sum up our whole discussion. We began by distinguishing two sorts of knowledge of objects, namely, knowledge by *acquaintance* and knowledge by *description*. Of these it is only the former that brings the object itself before the mind. We have acquaintance with sense-data, with many universals, and possibly with ourselves, but not with physical objects or other minds. We have *descriptive* knowledge of an object when we know that it is *the* object having some property or properties with which we are acquainted; that is to say, when we know that the property or properties in question belong to one object and no more, we are said to have knowledge of that one object by description, whether or not we are acquainted with the object. Our knowledge of physical objects and of other minds is only knowledge by description, the descriptions involved being usually such as involve sense-data. All propositions intelligible to us, whether or not they primarily concern things only known to us by description, are composed wholly of constituents with which we are acquainted, for a constituent with which we are not acquainted is unintelligible to us. A judgment, we found, is not composed of mental constituents called "ideas," but consists of an occurrence whose constituents are a mind[49] and certain objects, particulars or universals. (One at least must be a universal.) When a judgment is rightly analysed, the objects which are constituents of it must all be objects with which the mind which is a constituent of it is acquainted. This conclusion forces us to analyse descriptive phrases occurring in propositions, and to say that the objects denoted by such phrases are not constituents of judgments in which such phrases occur (unless these objects are explicitly mentioned). This leads us to the view (recommended also on purely logical grounds) that when we say "the author of Marmion was the author of Waverley," Scott himself is not a constituent of our judgment, and that the judgment cannot be explained by saying that it affirms identity of denotation with diversity of meaning. It also, plainly, does not assert identity of meaning. Such judgments, therefore, can only be analysed by breaking up the descriptive phrases, introducing a variable, and making propositional functions the ultimate subjects. In fact, "the so-and-so is such-and-such" will mean that "x is so-and-so and nothing else is, and x is such-and-such" is capable of truth. The analysis of such judgments involves many fresh problems, but the discussion of these problems is not undertaken in the present paper.

Footnotes

[40] See references later.

[41] *Philosophical Essays*, "The Nature of Truth." I have been persuaded by Mr. Wittgenstein that this theory is somewhat unduly simple, but the modification which I believe it to require does not affect the above argument [1917].

[42] Cf. Meinong, *Ueber Annahmen, passim*. I formerly supposed, contrary to Meinong's view, that the relationship of supposing might be merely that of presentation. In this view I now think I was mistaken, and Meinong is right. But my present view depends upon the theory that both in judgment and in assumption there is no single Objective, but the several constituents of the judgment or assumption are in a many-term relation to the mind.

[43] This view has been recently advocated by Miss E.E.C. Jones. "A New Law of Thought and its Implications," *Mind*, January, 1911.

[44] I should now exclude "I" from proper names in the strict sense, and retain only "this" [1917].

[45] Meinong, *Ueber Annahmen*, 2nd ed., Leipzig, 1910, p. 141.

[46] *Mind*, July, 1910, p. 380.

[47] *Mind*, July, 1910, p. 379.

[48] The theory which I am advocating is set forth fully, with the logical grounds in its favour, in *Principia Mathematica*, Vol. I. Introduction, Chap. III; also, less fully, in *Mind*, October, 1905.

[49] I use this phrase merely to denote the something psychological which enters into judgment, without intending to prejudge the question as to what this something is.